What is True Success?

Exploring Answers from the Teachings of Seventh-Century Saint

Ali bin Abu Talib (p)

Excerpts from *Peak of Eloquence*
(Nahjul Balagha)

Edited by

Dr. Syed H. Akhtar

Email: truesuccess12@gmail.com

Available in Paperback or E-book
At www.Amazon.com
Also available at www.createspace.com/3573531;
www.Barnesandnoble.com and at
your local bookstore

God- Spirituality

ISBN-10: 1461014530
EAN-13: 9781461014539

Library of Congress Control Number: 2011904582
Createspace, North Charleston, SC

Tributes to Imam Ali (peace be upon him) by Scholars and Historians

"As for this young Ali, one cannot but like him.... Brave as a lion; yet with a grace, a truth, and affection worthy of a Christian knighthood."
Thomas Carlyle

"He united the qualifications of a poet, a soldier, and a saint; his wisdom still breathes in a collection of moral and religious sayings."
Sir Edward Gibbon

"He had contempt of the world, its glory and pomp; he feared God much, gave much alms, was just in all his actions humble and affable."
Dr. Henry Stubble

"His talents as an orator and his intrepidity (fearlessness) as a warrior were grateful to a nation in whose judgment courage was virtue and eloquence was wisdom."
Charles Mills

"His mother was delivered of him at Mecca (in Kaba), in the very Temple itself; which never happened to anyone else."
Simon Ockley

"He possessed the three qualities most prized by the Arabs: courage, eloquence, and munificence."
Washington Irving

"With him perished the truest hearted and best Moslem of whom Mohammadan history had preserved the remembrance."
Robert Durey Osborn

[For more information on this subject, refer to "Statements of scholars and historians about Imam Ali," Appendix B page 219]

A Glimpse at Some of the Wise Sayings of Ali bin Abu Talib (p)

- Giving relief to the distressed and helping the oppressed are means for atonement for great sins.
- The best way to serve God is not to make a show of it.
- A virtuous person is better than the virtue, and a vicious person is worse than the vice.
- The best wealth is to give up excessive desires.
- A wise person thinks before he speaks, whereas a fool speaks before he thinks.
- The sin that makes you sad and repentant is liked by God more than the good deed that makes you vain.
- The Real (act of) forgiveness is to forgive while having power to punish.
- There is no greater wealth than wisdom and no greater poverty than ignorance. There is no greater heritage than good manners and no greater support than consultation.
- Patience is of two kinds; patience over what hurts you and patience against your (unfulfilled) desires.
- Wealth is the fountainhead of passions.
- Return greetings with greater warmth. Repay favor with what is more. The initiator of a favor deserves greater merit.
- The wiser a person, the less he talks.
- Every breath of yours is one more step towards death.
- I wonder at the person who loses hope of salvation, while the door of repentance is still open.
- An advice: Do not lose hope in God's Mercy. At the same time do not take for granted immunity from His punishment.
- No wealth is more profitable than wisdom.

- No trait is more useful than politeness.
- No heritage is better than good manners.
- No eminence is greater than humility.
- I wonder at a miser who chooses to live like a destitute, but in the next world will have to give account like a rich person.
- I wonder at the arrogant and vain person. Yesterday he was only a lowly sperm, and tomorrow he will be a corpse.
- I wonder at the person who observes the universe created by God, yet doubts the existence of God.
- I wonder at the person who understands the marvel of the beginning of life, yet refuses to accept that he will be brought back to life again.
- I wonder at the man who takes great pains to decorate his temporary habitat (of this world), yet ignores his permanent abode (the Hereafter).
- This world is not a permanent abode. It is like a highway and you are a traveler.
- Loving one another is one-half of wisdom.
- One who agrees with the action of a group is regarded (by God) as having committed that action.
- Greed dulls the faculties of judgment and wisdom.
- Every blessing carries a right of God. If one fulfils that right, then the blessing increases, but if one falls short, the blessing might be lost.
- Anger is akin to madness, and the person usually repents; if not, then the madness is confirmed.
- God, the Glorified, has fixed the livelihood of the poor in the wealth of the affluent. Consequently, when a destitute one remains hungry, it is because some affluent person had denied him (his share). God, the Sublime, will question him (the affluent) about it.
- O people, Fear God; for a human is not created for naught, to waste oneself away, nor would be left unaccounted to commit nonsensical acts.

- Livelihood is of two kinds: The livelihood that you seek and the livelihood that seeks you. Even if you do not seek the latter, it will come to you.
- Words are in your control before you utter them, but once you have uttered, you are under their control. Therefore, guard your tongue as you guard your gold and silver. One expression may make you lose a blessing or invite punishment.
- Beware, wealth is a blessing; better is the health of the body, and (even) better than health of the body is purity of the heart.
- Lovers of God look at the inner side of things (while others look at the outer). They busy themselves with the lasting benefits (of the next world), while others seek immediate (worldly) benefits. They regard accumulation of wealth by others as a matter of lesser importance. They suppress those desires that they fear would hurt them (in the next world).

CONTENTS

WHAT IS TRUE SUCCESS?

DEDICATION

I dedicate this work primarily to the great personality of Imam Ali ibn Abu Talib (p), teacher, scholar, reformer, spiritual guide, moralist, jurist, administrator, ruler, military commander, friend of the poor and downtrodden, and much more. My father, the Late Dr. Syed Akhtar Ahmed, had done deep study of the book *Nahjul Balagha* or *Peak of Eloquence*. He was instrumental in drawing my attention to this valuable work at an early age.

ACKNOWLEDGMENTS

This work would not have been possible without the sincere help of many individuals. I thank Sheikh Jafar Muhibullah of Austin who, despite a busy schedule of doctoral studies, took time to look over the introductions to the chapters and provided useful suggestions, as well as provided encouragement for me to proceed with publication of this work. I owe thanks to Yahya Abu Haydar for his vast knowledge of Islamic topics, his expertise of Arabic language, and his help with authenticating translation of "Concept of God, His Oneness, and His Divine Attributes" and selected passages elsewhere. He also reviewed the manuscript at its completion. My son, Ali, helped in proofreading and editing the manuscript despite a busy Law practice. I am indebted to my nephew Ali Nasir Rizvi for his valuable advice.

Thanks go to the administrators of the Web site www.nahjulbalagha.com. The Web site was very useful in the present work. The book *Peak of Eloquence* (*Nahjul Balagha*), published by Tahrike Tarsile Qur'an, was also helpful.

Above all, I thank God Almighty for helping and guiding me in this long and difficult task.

ABBREVIATIONS

(s) The abbreviation represents "peace and blessings upon him and members of his family," as a token of respect. It will be used throughout the book wherever the name of Prophet Muhammad (s) is mentioned.

(p) The abbreviation represents "on him be peace" as a token of respect.

(pp) This abbreviation represents "Peace be upon them" as a token of respect when more than one Prophet or Imam is mentioned.

"A Saying" or "Saying of Imam Ali." This refers to his saying(s) taken from the book Nahjul Balagha, chapter titled "Selections from his sayings and preaching," which contains 489 of his sayings. These include his maxims as well as his replies to queries.

( ) Statements in parentheses are for explanation and are not part of the text.

EDITOR'S NOTE

The book in your hand is derived from an English translation of a collection of sermons, letters, and sayings of Imam Ali (p), which, in the original Arabic language is titled *Nahjul Balagha*, i.e., *Peak of Eloquence*. The sermons, letters, and sayings were delivered by Imam Ali during the six years of his Caliphate, as the ruler of the then Muslim State. Syed Mohammed Razi took it upon himself to collect these in the form of a book some one thousand years ago. It has been translated into many different languages. An English translation by Syed Ali Raza was published by Tahrike Tarsile Qur'an, Inc., of Elmhurst, New York. An online version is also available at www.nahjulbalagha.com.

The original collection consists of 239 sermons, seventy-nine letters, and 489 sayings. Each sermon deals with many topics, depending upon the needs of the time, in answer to a question, or in response to a specific event or request. The subjects deal with every aspect of worldly life and contain detailed guidance on moral values; God-consciousness; political, judicial, military, and administrative matters; the spiritual life; the life in the Hereafter; and other topics.

In the original text, the subject matter is scattered among many sermons and letters. Thus, one sermon may address more than one topic. If a reader wishes to know what more is said on a particular topic, then he/she will need to read the entire document.

There was a need for a topically arranged edition of the book. This void is, in some ways, filled by the book in your hand. Additionally, the topics selected are more relevant in the modern day and age, addressing the teachings of Imam Ali (p) that would be useful for humanity in day-to-day life.

We are told that God created humans to worship Him. In order to worship God we need to have understanding of who He is and who He is not. His worship with understanding paves the way for a God-conscious life and promise of a blissful life in the Hereafter, and this is true success.

The source of knowledge of Ali bin Abu Talib (p). Ali (p) did not receive any institutional or formal education. During his childhood years, the Prophet Muhammad (s) was his only teacher. Much of his adult life was spent in protecting the Prophet and fighting in the defensive wars against the enemy. The Prophet Muhammad himself was generally known as "unlettered", meaning he could not read or write. He claimed that his knowledge was imparted to him by Angel Gabriel and what he received through divine revelations from God Almighty.
(For more information on Imam Ali, please refer to his biography on page 215, Appendix A, and also see page 161.)

In this book, in the first section we learn some concepts about God, His wonderful creations and His bounties. The second section deals with leading a God-conscious life, which is a pre-requisite to true success. The third section deals with connecting with God through supplications. The last section contains his selected sayings and maxims replete with wisdom and guidance.

This is my humble effort, with full realization that I cannot improve upon the great work done by the earlier scholars. I pray to God Almighty that He forgive me for unintentional errors and lapses and that He accept this effort.

1. TO KNOW GOD

Concept of God, His Oneness, and His Divine Attributes

God's Bounties and Blessings

The Creation of Heaven, Earth, and Creation of Adam

CONCEPT OF GOD, HIS ONENESS AND HIS DIVINE ATTRIBUTES

Introduction: Imam Ali ibn Abu Talib (p) lived 1,400 years ago, during the advent of Islam in Arabia. He was a cousin of Prophet Muhammad (s), the Messenger of God. He was privileged to have the Prophet raise him in his own household and teach him. Additionally, he was a scholar of the Arabic language and had deep knowledge and understanding of the Qur'an.

The following is a collection of his various sermons and discourses on the concept of God. The sermons were delivered over several years. The excerpts are presented here in an abridged and topical format in modern English and rephrased where necessary. It is hoped that the reader will find this presentation enjoyable as well as enlightening.

His Praising and Glorifying God:
Praise is due to God, Whose worth cannot be described by the describer, Whose bounties cannot be counted by enumerators, and Whose claim cannot be fulfilled by those who attempt to do so. The height of intellectual courage cannot appreciate Him, and the depths of understanding cannot reach Him. For His description no limit has been laid down, no eulogy exists, no time is ordained, and no duration is fixed.
(Sermon 1)

Exalted is God, Whom the limits of endeavors cannot reach and intelligence cannot find. He is the First (having no beginning), having no limits, lest He would be confined within those limits. Nor does He have an end, such that He could cease (to exist).

(Sermon 93)

Praise be to God,Who is praised by all His creation,Whose hosts are overpowering, and Whose Exaltation is High. I praise Him for His successive favors and His abundant gifts. His forbearance is great, so that He forgives, and He is just in His decisions. He has knowledge of the present and the past. He designed the creation with knowledge, and brought it into existence with His unlimited capacity, without need for learning, without following any previous example, without committing any mistake, and without any help.

(Sermon 190)

Praise God, seeking completion of His Blessings, submitting to His Glory, and hoping for amnesty for disobeying Him. I invoke His help and I depend on Him alone. He whom He guides does not go astray; he who evokes His anger has no protection. Whomever He supports, he gets the needs fulfilled. He is the weightiest of all that is weighed and the most valuable of all that is treasured.

(Sermon 1)

O my God! Praise be to You for what You take and what You bestow; what You cure or with what You afflict; a Praise that is most acceptable to You, the most liked by You, and that is most dignified; a Praise which is equal to all Your creation; a Praise that reaches You and a Praise that is everlasting.

(Sermon 159)

His Advice to the People to Praise and Thank God:

I advise you, O people, to be God-conscious and to praise Him abundantly for His favors, bounties, and trials upon you. See how He chose you for His favors and dealt with you with Mercy. You committed sins openly, but He kept them hidden. You behaved in a way to incur His punishment, but He allowed you more time (to repent).

(Sermon 187)

Oneness and Uniqueness of God:

The foremost (duty) in religion is the acknowledgment of God; the perfection of acknowledging Him is to bear witness to Him; the perfection of bearing witness to Him is to believe in His Oneness; the perfection of believing in His Oneness is to regard Him as pure; and the perfection of regarding Him as pure is to deny Him attributes, because every attribute is a proof that it is different from that to which it is attributed, and everything to which something is attributed is different from the attribute.

Thus, whoever attempts a description of God creates His like; and whoever creates His like regards Him as two; and whoever regards Him as two recognizes parts for Him; and whoever recognizes parts for Him mistook Him; and whoever mistook Him faulted Him; and whoever faulted Him admitted limitations for Him; and whoever admitted limitations for Him enumerated Him (i.e., denied His oneness and uniqueness).

Whoever said, "In what is He?" held that He is confined; and whoever said, "On what is He?" held He is not on something else. He is a being, but not through the phenomenon of coming into existence. He exists, but not by coming out of nonexistence. He is near to everything, but not in physical proximity. He is distinct from everything, but not separated (by distance). He acts, but without the need of movement or need of instruments. He is One, such that there is none with whom He may keep company or none whose company He may miss.
(Sermon 1)

I stand witness that there is no god but God, the One. No one is like Him. (It is) a testimony that has been tested in its frankness, and its essence is our belief. We shall cling to it as long as we remain (alive), shall store it, facing the tribulations that overtake us, because it is the firm determination of belief, the first step towards good actions and Divine pleasure. It is the means to keep Satan away.
(Sermon 2)

He who assigns to Him (different) states does not believe in His Oneness; or he who likens Him (to any of His creation) has not grasped His reality. He who pictures Him in his imagination has meant (someone) other than God. He works but not with the help of tools. He assigns measures but not with the need of deliberation. He is rich but not through acquisition (of wealth).
(Sermon 185)

He is One, but not in a numerical sense. He is everlasting, without a limit. He exists, but without support. He is big, but not in a physical sense. He is big in position and great in authority.
(Sermon 184)

Divinely Revealed Attributes of God:
It is my belief that He is the First and He is the Manifest. I seek guidance from Him, as He is close (to me), and He is the Guide. I seek His help, as He is Mighty and He subdues (all troubles). I depend upon Him, as He is the Sufficer and the Supporter.
(Sermon 82)

Praise be to God, for Whom one condition does not precede another condition, such that He may be considered first or last, or He may be considered manifest before being hidden. Everyone enjoying honor is humble before God, and everyone (considered) powerful is weak compared to Him. Every owner is (in fact) owned by Him.

Everyone knowledgeable other than God is a learner (student). Everyone with skills may lose those abilities, except for Him. Everyone with hearing, except Him, is unable to hear faint and distant sounds, while loud sounds may make him deaf. Every seer, other than Him, is blind to hidden or tiny objects. Everything that He made manifest is insignificant compared to Him, and everything hidden by Him is incapable of becoming manifest.

What He created was not to fortify His authority, nor for fear of the consequences of (passage of) time, nor fearing some agitating peer, nor

any competing rival. Rather, all creatures are nourished by Him and are humbled (before Him). He is not inside anything, so that it may be said that He exists therein, nor is He separated from anything, so that it may be said that He is away from it. The act of creation did not fatigue Him, and no disability afflicted Him. No misgiving ever occurred to Him in His resolve. His verdict is certain, His wisdom is perfect, and His governance is overwhelming. He is sought at times of distress, and one needs to be God-conscious even when bounties abound.
(Sermon 64)

Praise be to God, who is High above all things, yet is near (to the creation) through His bounties. He is the Bestower of all rewards and distinctions, and Dispeller of all calamities and hardships. I praise Him for His compassionate generosity.
(Sermon 82)

Praise be to God, Who is not rich by withholding bounties, and Whose munificence and generosity do not make (Him) poor. Everyone who gives, loses (to that extent), except Him. He obliges through beneficial bounties and plentiful gifts. The whole creation is dependent on Him (for sustenance). He has guaranteed their livelihood and ordained their sustenance. He has prepared the way (to success) for those who turn to Him and those who seek what is with Him. He generously grants the requests and bestows bounties freely even when not requested. He is the First, such that nothing existed prior to Him. He is the Last, such that nothing will remain other than Him. He prevents the eyes from seeing or perceiving Him. (Passage of) time does not affect Him whatsoever, nor cause any change in Him. He is not in one particular place, to require Him to move (to another place).

He is so powerful that, when imagination shoots its arrows to comprehend the extent of His power, when the mind tries to reach Him in the depths of His realm, when the hearts long to grasp the realities of His attributes, and when intellect attempts to secure knowledge about His Being, crossing the pitfalls of the unknown, they would all be turned

back. They would return defeated, acknowledging that the reality of His essence cannot be grasped.
(Sermon 90)

He is the Creator, but not through activity or toil; He is the Hearer, but not by means of any physical organ; He is the Seer, but not by raising the eyelids; He is the Witness, but not by proximity; He is Distinct, but not by measurement; He is Manifest, but not by visualizing; and He is hidden, but not in a bodily sense. He is Distinct from things (created), because He overpowers them and dominates over them, while created things are distinct from Him because of their subjugation to Him and because they turn to Him.

God speaks, but not through speech and without the need of a tongue. He hears, but without the need of ears or listening aids. He remembers, but does not need to memorize. He determines, but without the need of mental faculties. He loves but without suffering sentimentally. He entertains dislikes and gets angry without experiencing emotion or pain.
(Sermon 185)

About His Might, Greatness, Sublimity, and Omniscience:
Praise be to God, Who pervades all hidden affairs, and towards Whom all manifest things point. He cannot be seen by the eye of a seer, but the eye, which does not see Him, cannot deny Him, while the mind that proves His existence cannot perceive Him. He is so high in sublimity that nothing can be more sublime than He, while in nearness, He is so near that no one can be nearer than He. However, his sublimity does not distance Him from anything of His creation, nor does His nearness bring them on an equal level to Him. He has not informed the (human) intellect about the extent of His qualities. Nevertheless, He has not prevented it from securing essential knowledge of Him. Therefore, He is such that all signs of existence bear proof of Him, until the denying mind also believes in Him. God is sublime beyond what is described by those who compare Him to things, or those who reject Him.
(Sermon 47)

Everything submits to Him and everything exists because of Him. He is the wealth of the poor, the honor of the lowly, the energy of the weak, and the shelter of the oppressed. Whoever speaks, He hears him, and whoever does not speak, He knows his secrets. The livelihood of everyone depends on Him, and to Him everyone will return.

(O God!) The eyes have not seen You, but You existed before Your describers were created. You did not create (the whole of creation) due to (any feeling of) loneliness, nor did You make them for any gain. He whom You apprehend cannot escape You. He, who disobeys You, does not decrease Your authority, and he, who obeys You, does not add to Your authority. He who disagrees with Your judgment cannot change it, and he who turns away from Your command cannot do without You. Every secret is manifest to You, and everything unknown (to others) is known to You.
(Sermon 108)

If He (God) gives away all that the mines of the earth contain, the treasures in the mountains, the gold, the silver, pearls, and coral from the oceans, it would not affect His munificence, nor diminish what He possesses. He has such treasures and bounties, which will not decrease by providing for the demands of the creatures. He is such a generous being, Whom giving to the beseechers does not diminish (His bounties), nor does the persistent asking of beseechers makes Him frugal (tightfisted).
(Sermon 90)

This world and the next world have submitted to Him, and the skies and earth have surrendered to Him as well. The trees worship Him (unknown to man) in the morning and evening, fire is produced from them (by His Will), and they produce ripe fruits (by His Will).
(Sermon 132)

Praise be to God who has displayed His Authority, Glory, Sublimity, and Might through the wonders of His creation, that dazzle the eyes and the minds, that are far removed from appreciating the reality of His at-

tributes. I stand witness that there is no god but God by virtue of belief, certainty, sincerity, and conviction.
(Sermon 197)

He joins diverse things and separates things that are joined together. He is not confined by any limits (of time and space). He is far beyond the sight of the seers.
(Sermon 185)

Presence or lack of motion does not occur in Him; how can it? It is He who has caused motion to come into existence. How could He be subjected to something that He himself set in motion? How could something appear in Him that He himself created? Had it been so, He would be subject to diversity, His Being would have become divisible (into parts), and His reality would have been prevented from being Eternal. If He had a front, then He would also have a back. He is far above being affected by things that affect (those) other than Him.
(Sermon 185)

God is aware of the calls of the beasts in the forests, the sins that people commit in privacy, the movement of the fish in the depths of ocean, and the rising of the water by tempestuous winds.
(Sermon 197)

Had they pondered over the greatness of His power and the vastness of His bounties, they would have returned to the right path (of acknowledging Him as God) and would fear the punishment (for rejecting Him), but hearts are afflicted and eyes are closed. Do they not see the tiny creatures He brought into existence, how He strengthened their bodily functions, gave them hearing, sight, made their body parts, and their tiny and delicate bodies?
(Sermon 184)

He brought into existence His creation without (following) any example, and He did not need any assistance.

He created the earth and suspended it without effort, held it in position without support, raised it without pillars, and protected it against destruction. He fixed mountains on it like pegs, solidified the rocks, caused streams to flow, and opened wide valleys. Whatever He made did not suffer from any flaw.

When He intends to create something, He says to it, "Be!" and "It is," but this is not through a voice that strikes (the ears). The act of creation was through His Word, "Be!" and it was.
(Sermon 185)

Praise be to God Who is recognized without being seen and Who creates without experiencing any difficulty. The monarchs submit to Him, acknowledging His Might.

He exercises superiority over the great and mighty through His generosity. It is He who made His creation to populate the earth and sent His messengers to warn of pitfalls, to present good examples, to advise them (the people) of their shortcomings. The messengers came to warn (humanity) about what is lawful and what is unlawful, the reward and punishment (i.e., Heaven and Hell) of God for the obedient and the rebellious, respectively. I praise Him, for He likes His creation to praise Him. He has fixed for everything a measure, for every measure set a time limit, and for every time limit there is documentation.
(Sermon 182)

About God's Knowledge:
His knowledge does not leave anything (outside His realm); it is (preserved) in a document which does not omit anything. We believe in Him, like the belief of one who has seen Him (through eyes of the heart) and has secured the promised rewards (of the Hereafter); a belief, the purity of which keeps one away from associating partners with God, and a belief with conviction that removes all doubts.
(Sermon 113)

His knowledge is without learning from anyone, and He ordains all matters without (the need of) reflection upon it or pondering.
(Sermon 212)

He is not preoccupied by (attending to) any matter. The passage of time does not bring any change in Him, He is not confined to any one place, and the tongues are unable to describe Him. The number of drops of water (in the ocean), the number of stars in the sky, or the (whereabouts of the) currents of winds are known to Him; so are the movements of ants on the rocks, or the resting place of grubs in the dark night. He possesses the knowledge of the place where the leaves fall, and He is aware of the stealthy movements of the eyes.
(Sermon 177)

Therefore, God alone knows what is there in the wombs, whether male or female, ugly or handsome, generous or miserly, mischievous or pious, and who will be doomed to Hell and who will be in the company of the Prophets in Paradise. The knowledge of the hidden things[1] is not known to anyone, save God, except the knowledge that God passed on to Prophet Muhammad (s).

[Note: Imam Ali also said that he had that knowledge that was transmitted to him by the Prophet (s).]
(Sermon 12)

God, the Glorified and Sublime; nothing is hidden from Him of whatever people do in their nights or days. He knows all the details, and His knowledge covers them. Your limbs are a witness, the organs of your body constitute an army (against yourself), your inner self serves Him as eyes (to witness your wrongdoings), and (even) when you are alone, He is with you.
(Sermon 198)

---

1 The knowledge of hidden things means knowledge of the Day of Judgment, as explained in this verse: *"Verily, God is He with Whom is the knowledge of the Hour..."* Qur'an 31:34.

God Did Not Give Birth to a Son, nor was He Born of Anyone:

He does not have a form, and thus there is no possibility of any change whatsoever. He did not beget, such that He would be considered to have been begotten. In that case, He would be subject to limitations. He is too exalted to have a son. He is too sublime to have consorts. Human imagination, perception, and senses cannot reach His essence. One cannot assign Him a numerical quantity. He is beyond understanding and beyond imagination. He does not pass from one state to another. Passage of nights and days do not cause Him to age. Light and darkness do not affect Him.

(Sermon 185)

God Will Bring an End to This World, and Then Resurrect as He Wills:

He will end the earth, as it presently exists, so that everything on it will become nonexistent.

Bringing end to the world after its creation would not be anything strange (for Him) any more than was its initial construction. How could it be?

Even if all His creation, including all humanity, using their intellect, were to join forces to create (even) a single mosquito, they would not be able to do so. They would be bewildered and frustrated. Their plans and powers would fail, and they would end up disappointed and tired, acknowledging their failure, admitting their inability to accomplish it, and realizing that they were too weak (even) to destroy it (the mosquito) against God's will.

Surely, after the end of the world, God the Glorified will remain alone with nothing else except Him. He will remain after the extinction of the world, just as He was before its creation. At that moment, time, periods, places, and intervals would cease to exist. There will remain absolutely nothing except God, the One and the All-Powerful. To Him is the return of all things. The creation was not due to its own power, and prevention of its extinction is not in its power either. If any of the creation had the power to prevent its own destruction, then it would have continued to exist indefinitely.

When He made a thing, the creation of it did not cause Him any difficulty, and the act of creation did not fatigue Him. He did not create in order to increase His authority nor for any fear of loss or harm, nor to seek help against an overwhelming foe, nor to guard against any adversary, nor to extend His domain, nor because He felt lonely and desired to seek company.

He will end all the creation, not because of any worry that has overcome Him in regards to its upkeep and administration, nor because He will derive any pleasure from it. The (long) duration of earth's existence does not make Him weary. However, God the Glorified has nurtured it with His kindness, kept it intact with His command, and perfected it with His power. Then after its destruction, He will resurrect it, but not because He needed it, nor to attain any honor or power.
(Sermon 185)

God's Mercy, Forgiveness, and Bounties:
Praise is due to God in Whose Mercy no one loses hope, of Whose Bounty no one is deprived, in Whose Forgiveness, no one is overlooked, and for Whose worship no one is too great. His Mercy never ceases and His Bounty is never exhausted.
(Sermon 45)

Know, O creatures of God, that He has not created you for nothing, and has not left you (completely) free. He knows the extent of His favors and the amount of His bounties to you. Therefore, ask Him for success and for the attainment of your desires. Beseech Him and invoke His generosity. No curtain hides you from Him, nor is any door (of communication) closed between you and Him. He is present at every place, at all times, and in every moment. He is (at all times) with

every human and jinn[1] kind. Giving does not cause diminution of His bounties.
(Sermon 194)

About God's Eternity:
I stand witness that there is no god but God; He is One, and He has no partner; He is the First, such that nothing existed before Him; He is the Last (Eternal), such that there is no End to His existence. Division or splitting into parts of His entity is not possible. Hearts cannot comprehend His nature. Eyes cannot envision Him.
(Sermon 84)

Praise be to God, Who existed from before the coming into existence of the seat of His throne (the universe), the sky, the earth, the jinn, or the human beings. He cannot be perceived by imagination nor measured by understanding. He who begs from Him does not divert His attention (from others), nor does giving away cause Him diminution (in His bounties). He does not see by means of an eye, nor can He be confined to a particular place. He cannot be said to have companions. He does not create with (the help of) limbs. He cannot be perceived by senses. His being is beyond the estimation of humans.
(Sermon 181)

His Being preceded (the creation of) time. He existed when nothing existed (whatsoever); this is an indication that He is above them all. By His creating the sense organs, it is clear that He has no need of such sense organs. By the (existence of) opposites in His creation, it becomes known that He does not have an opposite, and by the existence of similarities among the created things, it becomes known that there is nothing in His creation that is similar to Him. He has made the light opposite of the darkness; the brightness opposite of the gloom; the dryness opposite of the moisture; and the heat opposite of the cold. He causes affinity among antagonistic things.

---

1 Creatures made of fire, hidden from humans. Satan belongs to this type of being.

It cannot be said that He came into being after He had been in non-existence, because in that case the attributes of the created things would be assigned to Him; there would then remain no difference between Him and His creation, and He would then have no clear distinction over His creation. Thus, the Creator and the created would be on an equal footing, and the Initiator and the initiated would be considered at the same level.

(Sermon 185)

GOD'S BOUNTIES AND BLESSINGS

Introduction: Our bodies, the faculties of sight, speech, smell, and hearing, are a gift from God to us. Our bodily functions, the physiology, the chemistry, the circulation, etc. are gifts from God to us. Our intellect, knowledge, power of reasoning, and our faith are His gifts. Our parents, offspring, kin, friends, etc., are His gifts to us. Our environment, the ecosystem, the sun, the moon, the solar system, and everything that makes our little planet livable are His gifts. All of them, and many more beyond our knowledge, are bounties of God to humankind. We lack the ability to understand, count, or thank Him for all His bounties. What follows is Imam Ali's (p) unique perspective in acknowledging and seeking the bounties of God, while at the same time not overlooking our final abode, the Hereafter.

Reminding People of God's Bounties:
God has made ears to (listen and) remember what is important, made eyes to see (the truth) instead of remaining blind (to the truth). **(Sermon 80)**

He has provided you sustenance, surrounded you with His knowledge, promised rewards, and has bestowed upon you bounties and gifts. **(Sermon 82)**

God, the Creator and Provider:
Praise be to God, who is acknowledged but without being seen, Who creates without needing to ponder, and Who is Ever Existent. He was there when no sky or heaven existed, nor a gloomy night, nor a peaceful ocean, nor mountains with broad pathways, nor earth with plains

and fields, nor any creatures. He is the Originator of all creation, its Master, Owner, and Provider. The sun and the moon move (obediently) according to His will (His laws).

He distributes sustenance, keeps count of the deeds, and keeps count (even) of breaths. He is aware of stealthy glances and what is hidden in the bosoms. He knows the places of stay (of His subjects) in the loins (of the fathers) and in the wombs (of the mothers), and when they reach life's end (the resting place of the soul).
(Sermon 89)

Share Your Bounties and Pray for More (Advice to His Son):
If you find around you such poor, needy, and destitute people who are willing to carry your load (i.e., burden of your wealth) for you, as far as to the Day of Judgment, then consider this a blessing. Engage them and pass your burden on to them, i.e., distribute your wealth amongst the poor, destitute, and the needy. Help others to the best of your ability, and be kind and sympathetic to fellow human beings. Thus, relieve yourself from the heavy responsibility and liability of having to submit an account on the Day of Judgment of how you have made use of the bounties. Thus, you may arrive at the end of the journey (i.e., the afterlife) light and fresh, and have enough provision (in store) for you there (i.e., rewards for having done your duty to God and humanity in your worldly life).

Think it over, that by simply granting you the privilege of praying to Him for favors and mercies, He has handed over to you the keys of His treasures. Whenever you are in need, you should pray, and He will confer His bounties and blessings.
(Letter 31)

Verily, it (death) will come to you as the most important and the greatest event of your life; it might carry blessings and rewards for you, or it might bring in its wake punishments and sufferings. It is for you to decide whether to proceed towards perpetual peace and **blessings, i.e.,** Paradise, or towards eternal damnation, i.e., Hell.
(Letter 27)

Prayers for God's Bounties:

Praise be to God, whose bounty never misses and whose favors cannot be repaid.
(Sermon 48)

They (the servants of God) are allowed time to seek deliverance, shown the right path, and allowed to live (on earth) and seek (His) **favors**. The darkness of doubts has been removed from them, and they are let free in this period of life as a training place in order to make preparation for the Day of Judgment, to search for the objective with thoughtfulness, to secure benefits and provision for the place of (everlasting) stay (the next world).
(Sermon 82)

Praise be to God to Whom is the return of all created beings and the end of all matters. We render Him praise for the greatness of His generosity, the charity of His proofs, the increase of His bounties and favors, a praise which may fulfill His rights, repay Him with thanks, take (us) near His rewards (of the Hereafter), and that will increase in His kindnesses.
(Sermon 181)

THE CREATION OF HEAVEN, EARTH, AND CREATION OF ADAM

Introduction: God brought forth His creation out of nothing. The animals, the flora, the fauna, the insects, the microbes, the elements of nature, all were created for our benefit. God says in the Scripture[1] that He subjected the sun, the moon, and the cattle to us, and He instructs us to glorify and thank Him in return. Imam Ali (p) enumerates here some of the creations, examines them from his perspective, expresses wonderment, and sends praises and gratitude to God in beautiful words. It is truly amazing that Imam Ali (p) made statements regarding science, astronomy, biology, physics, and origin of life with details that were unknown to man 1400 years ago. Hundreds of years later science verified these statements.

---

1 God says: "He created the heavens and the earth with truth; exalted is He above what they associate (with Him). He created man (human) from a drop of sperm, and behold, he is an open disputer. He created cattle for you, wherein is warmth and many gains, and you eat thereof. There is comeliness in them for you when you drive them (home) and when you lead them forth (to pasture). They bear your loads to lands, which you could not otherwise reach but with distress; verily, your Lord is Compassionate, Merciful. (He made) horses, mules, and donkeys that you may ride upon them and as a finery (adornment); and He creates what you do not know. It rests upon God to make (show) the straight way, and among them (people) are deviating ones; if He pleases, he would certainly guide you all aright. He it is who sends down water from the heavens for you; from it you drink, and by it trees (and vegetations) grow on which you pasture your cattle. With this (rain) He produces corn, olives, palm, grapes, and all (types of) fruits for you; verily there is a sign in this for people who reflect. He made the night, the day, the sun, and the moon (that are) of use to you; and the stars have been made of service (to you) by His decree; verily, there are signs in this for people who understand" (Qur'an 16:3–12).

"He is (the One) Who made the sun a radiation (shining bright) and moon a light, and measured stations for it that you might know the number of years and the reckoning (of time)…" (Qur'an, 10:5).

"He it is Who made the stars for you that you may be rightly guided (in travel) in the land and the sea…" (Qur'an 6:97).

God brought forth creation through His Omnipotence, dispersed winds through His Compassion, and made firm the shaking earth with mountains.
(Sermon 1)

The Creation of the Universe:
He originated the creation most initially, without need of undergoing reflection, without use of any experiment, and without needing to make any movement. He allotted all created things their time limits, bestowed upon them their variations, features, and their properties. He possessed full knowledge of all of the creation before bringing it into existence, knew well their limits, confines, propensities, and intricacies.

When the Almighty created the openings in the atmosphere, the vastness of the firmament, and the strata of the winds, He made water to flow into it, whose waves were stormy and whose surges leapt one over the other. He loaded it on dashing winds and mighty typhoons, ordered them to shed it back (as rain), gave the winds control over the force of the rain, and designated its limitations. The wind blew under it while water flowed furiously over it. The Almighty God created the wind, designated its location, intensified its movement, and sent it everywhere. Then, He ordered the wind to raise up the deep waters and to intensify the waves of the oceans. Therefore, the wind churned it like the churning of curd, until its level was raised and the surface was covered with foam. Then the Almighty raised the foam up to the wind and the vast firmament, and made the seven heavens. He made the lower heaven a stationary surge and the upper heaven a protective ceiling without any pillars to support it or nails to hold it together. Then, He decorated the lowest heaven with stars and bright meteors, and then He suspended the shining sun and the shimmering moon, making the revolving heavens and rotating firmament.
(Sermon 1)

Greatness of God; the Creation of the Universe:
It is through God's greatness and His unique power of innovation that He made solid, dry earth out of the water of the fathomless, dashing ocean.

Then He made it into layers and separated them into seven heavens. Then they were made stationary (fixed their position) by His command. They were obedient to Him and submitted in awe and fear of Him.

He also created stones, rocks, hills, and lofty mountains. He put them in their respective positions and made them firm and stationary. Their peaks rose high above the earth, while their roots remained deep. In this way, He raised the mountains above the plains and fixed their foundations in the vast expanse underneath, wherever they stood. He made their peaks high and their bodies lofty. He made them like pegs deep into the earth. Consequently, the earth became stable; otherwise, its surface would give in, sink with its inhabitants, or move and shake.

Therefore, glorified is He who stabilized the earth, restrained the flowing waters, and solidified it. In this way, He made the earth a cradle for His creatures and spread it for them in the form of flat plains over the deep ocean. He made it steady, so it may not move. He made strong winds move the water, and made the clouds to draw up water from it.

"Verily in this there is a lesson for him who fears (God)." **(Qur'an 79:26)**
(Sermon 210)

More on the Creation of the Universe:
In creation, the big, the delicate, the heavy, the light, the strong, and the weak are all equally important. Similarly, the sky, the air, the winds, and the water are equally important. Therefore, look at the sun, the moon, the vegetation, the plants, the night, and the day. Observe the springing of the streams, the gigantic mountains, their high peaks, the diversity in nature, and the variety of languages. Then, woe be to him who disbelieves in the Creator. He who believes that there are fields but no cultivator, and there is no maker of the diverse shapes in creation, does not possess a logical argument for what he believes. Can a building be constructed without a builder?
(Sermon 184)

About Creation:

God originated creation without any prior example. He showed us the realm of His Might and demonstrated wonders that speak of His Wisdom. The proof of His creative power and His wisdom is in the wonderful things we see. His creation is an argument in His favor, and it guides us towards Him. Even an inanimate creation guides us towards Him, as though it "speaks" in its silence.

(O God), I stand witness that he who imagines You with having limbs or a body does not have any knowledge of You, and his heart does not show conviction that You have no partner. Those who liken You to their idols and imagine you to wear apparel like creatures, they are in manifest error. I stand witness that whoever compares You with anything from Your creation makes an equal for You, and whoever does that is an unbeliever according to unambiguous verses and clear arguments in Your Book (The Qur'an). (I stand witness that) You are God, Who cannot be comprehended by the limit of (human) intelligence, nor do You suffer any change of condition or alteration of state by any stretch of the imagination.

(Sermon 90)

The Magnificence of Creation:

Praise be to God, the Creator of humankind. He spread the earth, He makes streams to flow, and He makes vegetation to grow. His primal existence has no beginning, nor does His eternity have an end. Foreheads bow to him and lips proclaim His Oneness. He set the limits of things at the time He created them. He kept Himself separate from any likeness (to His creation).

(Sermon 162)

Among the proofs of His creation is the creation of the heavens that are suspended without pillars and are stable without support. He beckoned them and they responded obediently and humbly with promptness. If they had not acknowledged His Godhood and obeyed His command, He would not have chosen them to be the place for

His throne, the abode of His angels, and the destination for the pure words and the righteous deeds of His creatures.

He has made the stars in the skies as signposts by which the travelers on the earth are guided. The gloom of the dark curtains of night does not block their light, nor do the veils of the dark night have the power to block the light of the moon when it spreads. Glory be to God, from Whom is not hidden low regions of the earth or the high mountains, even when the gloom of the dark night shrouds them. The thundering of clouds on the horizons of the skies, or the sparks of lightning in the clouds, or the falling of leaves blown away from their places by strong winds, or the downpour from the sky, they are not hidden from Him. He knows where the raindrops fall and where they collect, where the grubs leave behind their trails, or where they drag themselves. He knows what livelihood would suffice a mosquito, and what a female bears in the womb.
(Sermon 181)

About the Perfection in Creation:
God has fixed limits for everything He has created and made the limits firm, and He has fixed its working and made the working delicate. He has fixed its direction, and it does not transgress the limits of its position nor fall short of reaching the end of its aim. It did not disobey when commanded; how could it, since all matters are governed by His Will? He is the Creator of varieties of things without the use of imagination, without the urge of an impulse, without (the benefit of) any experiment, and without needing a partner who might have assisted Him in creating wonderful things.

Thus, creation was perfected by His order; it bowed in His obedience and responded to His call. The laziness of a slug (insect) or the inertness of an excuse-finder did not prevent it from responding to His call. Therefore, He straightened the things and fixed their limits. With His power, He created coherence in their contradictory aspects and joined those that were similar. Then, He separated them into varieties

that differ in sizes, quantities, properties, and shapes. He made them firm and gave them shape as He willed.
(Sermon 90)

A Description of the Creation of Adam:
God collected clay from hard, soft, sweet, and sour types of earth. Then He dipped it in water to purify it, and then kneaded it, adding moisture until it became gluey. From it, He carved an image with curves, joints, limbs, and segments. He solidified it until it dried up for a fixed time and a known duration. Then He blew into it of His Spirit, whereupon it took the form of a human being with a mind that governs him, an intellect that he makes use of, and limbs that serve him to change his position. He gave him wisdom that differentiates between truth and falsehood, and senses of taste and smell. He is a mixture of clays of different colors, cohesive materials, and differing properties like heat, cold, softness, and hardness.
(Sermon 1)

Creation of Man (continued):
Look at man, whom God has created in the dark wombs, behind layers of curtains (inside the abdomen of the mother), from a tiny sperm.[1] Then, He made it into a shapeless clot, then into an embryo, then a suckling infant, then a child, and finally a man. He gave him a heart, a tongue to talk, and eyes to see with, so that he may take lesson (from whatever is around him) and reflect upon it, and pay heed to warning, and thereby abstain from evil.
(Sermon 82)

More on Man's Creation:
O creature, who has been fairly created and who has been nurtured and cared for in the darkness of the womb! You were originated with the essence of clay and deposited in a quiet place for a known length

1 "He (God) creates you in the wombs of your mothers, one creation after another, in triple (layers of) darkness (abdominal wall, placenta, amniotic membrane)" (Qur'an 39:6).

and a fixed term.[1] You moved within the womb of your mother as an embryo, neither responding to a call nor hearing any voice.

Then, you were taken out from your place of stay to a place you had not been, and you did not have knowledge of the awaiting benefits. You were not aware as to who guided you to obtain nourishment from the breast of your mother. He who is unable to comprehend the intricacies of a physical being certainly cannot comprehend the (sublime) nature of the Creator.

(Sermon 162)

On the Creation of the First Man and the Deputation of the Prophets:

When God had spread out the earth and enforced His commands, He chose Adam (peace be upon him) as the best of all of His creation. He made him to reside in Paradise and arranged for his sustenance, and He informed him of what was prohibited. He warned Adam that approaching the prohibited would be considered disobedience to God, and would jeopardize his status.

However, Adam disobeyed, and God knew it beforehand. Consequently, God sent him down to earth after (accepting) his repentance, in order to populate the earth with his (Adam's) progeny, and for him to serve as a prophet among His creatures.[2]

When God made Adam to die, He did not leave humankind without another person, who would serve as His proof and plea for His Godhood and be a link between humankind and God.

He ordained livelihoods, both plentiful and scarce. He distributed bounties sparingly as well as abundantly. He tested whomever He chose, with prosperity or with poverty, to know who was grateful and

---

1 "Did We not create you of a despicable fluid (semen)? Then placed it in a safe place (uterus) till the appointed term (of pregnancy)" (Qur'an 77:20–22).

2 God forgave Adam and Eve. God bestowed on them His Grace and pleasure before they were sent down to earth.

who was patient. He coupled affluence with destitution, safety with calamity, and pleasure with grief. He fixed their ages; some were long and others were short. He has ordained death for all.

He did not create from preexisting matter,[2] or from existing examples. He created whatever He intended and then He fixed its limits, and He shaped whatever He shaped and gave it the best shape. Obedience to Him is ordained; however, it is of no benefit to Him. He has knowledge of the past, the knowledge of the present, knowledge of what is in the high heavens, and what is (deep) in the earth.
(Sermon 90)

About Those Who are Misguided:

When a human being attains adulthood, he/she falls victim to self-conceit and becomes perplexed. He (a human) satisfies his desires, gets busy in fulfilling his wishes, and seeks the pleasures of the world. He does not fear the consequences of his deeds. He spends his short life in vain pursuits. He earns no rewards for the afterlife, nor does he fulfill obligations. Fatal illness overtakes him while he is still immersed in enjoyments, and he becomes perplexed. He passes the night in wakefulness due to grief and pain from the ailment. His relatives watch helplessly as he suffers the pangs of death. He dies burdened with his vices.
(Sermon 82)

About the Creation of the Ant:

Do they not see the tiny beings He has created; how He designed their systems, gave them hearing, sight, and made for them body parts? Look at the ant with its small body and delicate form; how it moves about and secures its livelihood. It carries the food grain to its hole in the earth and deposits it in place. It collects its sustenance during summer for use in winter. God has guaranteed its livelihood. God, Kind is He, does not overlook its needs and does not deprive it of

---

2 God originated creation from nothing. He brought matter into existence from nonexistence.

its sustenance. If you ponder over its anatomy and physiology, and its eyes on its head, you would be amazed at its creation.

Exalted is God, Who made it stand on its legs. No one helped Him in its origination and no one assisted Him in its creation. The reaches of your imagination will not grasp knowledge about Him, except that you will realize that the Originator of the ant is the same as the Originator of the date palm. God created everything with intricate details, and all living beings have a similar origin.
(Sermon 184)

About the Creation of the Bat:
An example of His delicate and wonderful creation and great wisdom is seen in bats. They stay hidden in the daylight, although daylight reveals everything else. They are active in the night, whereas other creatures rest at night. Their eyes are dazed by the daylight. God has confined them to their places of hiding instead of going out in the daytime. Consequently, they shut their eyes in the day, treat night as a lamp, and forage in search of their livelihood. The darkness of night does not hinder their eyesight, nor does the gloom of darkness prevent them from flight. They obtain their sustenance at night. Glorified is He who has made the night as "day" for bats to seek livelihood and made the day for them to rest and sleep. He has given them wings without feathers. You can see the veins in the wings quite distinctly. The two wings are delicate yet sturdy, and just right for them to fly. When they fly, their young ones hang on to them for protection. The young stays with the parent wherever it goes, and does not leave until it becomes strong enough for flying. Glorified is God, Who creates everything (unique) without any precedent.
(Sermon 154)

About the Creation of the Peacock and Creation of Birds:
God has accomplished wonderful creations, including the living, the lifeless, the stationary, and the moving. He has established such clear proofs for His fine creative power and His Might that minds submit to Him in acknowledgment. His creation is proof of His Oneness. He

has created birds of various colors and shapes that live in the burrows of the earth, in the openings of high passes, and on the peaks of mountains. They fly by God's permission. They flutter with their wings in the expanse of the open atmosphere. God brought them into existence from nonexistence. (He gave some of them) exotic shapes, and fashioned their bones and joints and covered them with flesh. He prevented some of them from flying easily in the sky because of their heavy bodies and allowed them to use their wings only close to the ground. He has set them in different colors by His Might and exquisite creative power.

The most amazing among them is the creation of the peacock. God created its male in the most symmetrical shape, gave it a variety of hues, and set them in attractive design. Its tail is (unusually) long. When it is close to the female, it spreads out its folded tail and raises it up to cast a shade over its head, as if it were the sail of a boat. It feels proud of its colorful tail and swaggers with its movements.

I am telling you all this from (my own) observation. You would imagine its feathers to be sticks made of silver and the wonderful circles and sun-shaped design thereon to be of pure gold and of green emerald. They resemble a bouquet of flowers. If you likened them to ornaments, then they would be like gems of different color, studded in silver.

The peacock walks with vanity and pride, and throws open its tail and wings, self-admiring the handsomeness of its dress and the hues of its necklace of gems. On the crown of its head, there is a bunch of green variegated feathers. Its neck begins in the shape of a goblet and the stretch up to its belly is as the hair dye of Yemen in color, or like silk cloth put on a polished mirror that looks as if it has been covered with a black veil. Because of its excessive luster and extreme brightness, it appears that a lush green color has been mixed with it. Along the openings of its ears, there is a line of shining bright daisy color like the thin end of a pen. Whiteness shines on the black background. There is hardly a hue that it does not have, its surface is polished, and its appearance is bright and silken. It is therefore like scattered blossoms that have not been seasoned by the rains of spring or the sunshine of summer. However, when it casts its glance at its legs, it bemoans, displaying grief, because its legs are thin like the legs of Indo-Persian crossbred cocks. At the end of its shin, there is a thorn (-like projection).

It also sheds its plumage and puts off its dress. They all fall away but grow again. They fall away like the falling of leaves from twigs, and then they begin to grow until they return to the state that existed before their shedding. The new hues match the previous ones, and all the colors are restored like the original. If you carefully examine its feather, it would appear like a red rose, surrounded by emerald green and then golden yellow in color.
(Sermon 164)

A Description of the Locust:
God gave the locust two red eyes with two moonlike pupils, gave it tiny ears, fashioned for it a mouth, gave it two teeth for cutting, and two sickle like feet to grip with them. The farmers are afraid of locusts for their crops, because when they attack the fields (usually in large numbers); they gobble up the crop, despite the tiny size of the insect. The farmers are usually unable to drive them away.
(Sermon 184)

2. TO LIVE A GOD-CONSCIOUS LIFE

ADVICE FOR SUCCESSFUL LIFE TO HIS SON

(Excerpts from Letter No. 31)

Introduction: The following excerpts are from the profound advice given by Imam Ali (p) to his son. This advice covers many aspects of life, the relationship with God, the method of supplicating to God, behavior with other people (emphasizing family, neighbors, friends, even foes), and preparing for the life in the Hereafter. The impeccable character of Imam Ali, his spiritual excellence, his relationship with God, his struggle for justice, and his hard-earned lessons of life are evident from this advice. He practiced every bit of what he preached. This document is bound to leave a deep impression on the reader.

Importance of God-Consciousness:
My first and foremost advice to you, My Son, is to be God-conscious. Be His obedient servant. Keep the thought of Him always fresh in your mind. Be attached to and carefully guard the principles of Islam (submission to God) that connect you with God. Can any other connection be stronger, more durable, and more lasting than this, so that you may command greater respect and consideration from God?

Accept good exhortations (advice) and refresh your mind with them. Adopt God-consciousness and overcome your excessive desires with its help. Build your character with the help of true faith in religion and God.

As you are a noble, virtuous, and pious young man, I am confident that you will receive Divine Guidance and Succour. I firmly believe that God will help you to achieve your aims in life. I ask you to make a promise to yourself to follow my advice carefully.

The Creator is also the Annihilator. The One who annihilates has the power to bring everything back again into existence. The One who sends calamities also has the power to protect you from the calamities.

Remember, My Son, had there been any other god besides the One True God, he (the other) would have also sent his (own) prophets, and they would have pointed out to humankind the domain and glory of the other god. Nothing like that has occurred. He is the One True God, Whom all should acknowledge and worship. He has explained this Himself (in the Qur'an). Nobody is a partner with Him in His Domain, Might, and Glory. He is Eternal, He has always been that way, and He shall always remain as such.

He existed before the universe came into being. His Existence is without a beginning. He shall remain when every other thing (in His creation) shall perish. His Existence is without end. God's Glory and His Existence are preeminent, transcendent, and incomparable. He is beyond the grasp of (human) intellect. No one has the ability to understand or visualize God.

When you have accepted these facts, then your behavior should be like that of a person who realizes that his own status, power, and position are nothing compared to that of the Lord. You would want to be the one who desires to gain His Blessings through prayers and obedience, the one who fears His wrath and His punishments and who is absolutely in need of His help and protection. Remember, My Son, God has not ordered you to do anything but that which is good and which propagates goodness, and He has not prohibited you from anything except that which is evil and which will lead to bad consequences.

Remember, My Son, the best of my advices to you is to be God-conscious, to perform the duties made incumbent upon you by God, and to follow in the footsteps of your (noble and pious) ancestors and relatives. Verily, they carefully evaluated their thoughts and deeds, and they carefully evaluated before saying anything, or before taking an action. I advise you to follow their example.

How to Pray to God for Your Needs:

Do not seek help or protection from anybody but God. Reserve your prayers, your requests, and your solicitations for God only, because to withhold, to deprive, and to deny lies in His Power alone.

Therefore, the best thing for you is to seek guidance from the One who has created you, Who maintains and nourishes you, Who has given you a balanced mind and a normally working body. Your invocations should be reserved for Him alone, your requests and solicitations should be to Him alone, and you should only fear Him.

Realize this truth, my son, that the Lord, who owns and holds the treasures of heaven and the earth, has given you permission to ask and to beg (Him) for them, and He has promised to grant your prayers.[1] He has told you to pray for His favors, that He may grant them to you, and to ask for His Blessings, that He may bestow them upon you. God has not appointed guards to prevent your prayers from reaching Him, nor is there any need for anybody to intercede with Him on your behalf.

He hears you whenever you call Him and accepts your prayer whenever you pray to Him. Invoke God to grant you your heart's desire, lay before Him the secrets of your heart, tell Him about all the calamities that have befallen you, the misfortunes that face you, and beseech His help to overcome them. Invoke God's help and support in all difficulties and distresses.

Remember that the little that is granted to you by God will be more useful, honorable, and respectable for you than what is granted by a human (even if it is) in abundance. What can a human give you, but only that which is from God?

---

1 "Your Lord says: "Call unto Me, I will answer you" (Qur'an 40: 60).

You may implore Him to grant you long life and sound health; you may pray to Him for prosperity; you may request Him for such favors and grants that none but He (alone) can bestow.

Think over it, that by simply granting you the privilege of praying to Him for His favors and mercies, He has handed over the keys of His treasures to you. Whenever you are in need, you should pray, and He will confer His bounties and blessings (on you). Sometimes you will find that your requests are not immediately granted, but you need not be disappointed, because the granting of prayers often rests with the true purpose and intention of the seeker. Sometimes the prayers are delayed because the Merciful Lord wants you to receive further rewards for patiently bearing calamities and sufferings, to continue to believe sincerely in (receiving) His help. Thus, you may be awarded better favors than you had requested.

Sometimes your prayers are turned down; this may be to your benefit, because you often unknowingly ask for things that are harmful to you. If your requests are granted, then they will do you more harm than good, and many of your requests may be such that, if they are answered, they will result in your eternal damnation. Thus, the refusal to answer your solicitations is a blessing in disguise. Therefore, you should be very careful in asking God for His favors. Pray for such things that are beneficial to you. Remember, my dear Son, that wealth and power (if you pray for them) are such things that they will not always remain with you and they may bring you harm in the life Hereafter.

Know, My Son, that you cannot have every wish of yours granted. You cannot expect to escape from death. Therefore, be realistic in your expectations, desires, and cravings. Be reasonable (and realistic) in making requests.

Virtues of Patience:

Develop the virtue of patience against sufferings, calamities, and adversities. Patience is one of the highest forms of morality, nobility, and it is the best trait one can acquire. Put trust in God and seek His protection in every calamity and suffering, because you will thereby entrust yourself and your affairs to the best Trustee and to the mightiest Guardian.

Life of This World:

Those who have carefully studied the life of this world, they spend their days as if they know that they are travelers here who have to leave a place that is famine-stricken, unwholesome, and (often) unfriendly. They know that they have to proceed towards lands (of the next world) which are fertile, congenial, where there are abundant provisions, comforts, and pleasures. They have eagerly embarked on the journey. They feel happy, cherishing the hope of future blessings and (eternal) peace. They have willingly accepted the sufferings, troubles, and the hazards of the way (in this world), the parting with friends, scarcity of food, and lack of comfort during the journey (in this world), so that they may reach the destination (Paradise), a happy place. They do not resent bearing hardships, and they do not begrudge giving charity and assistance to the poor and the needy.

Each step they take towards their goal, tiring and exhausting as it may be, is a happy event in their lives.

On the contrary, the people who are attached to this world are sadly engulfed in its short-lived, fast-fading, and depraved pleasures. They are like travelers who are in a fertile and happy region and they know that the journey they have to undertake will lead them to an arid and infertile land. Could anything be more loathsome and abhorrent than the journey of theirs?

Nothing in this world is (truly) useful to you, unless it has some utility and value in the next world. If you lament over things that you have lost in this world, then worry much more about the loss of things of eternal benefit (in the Hereafter). Your past, and with it most of what was in your possession, has departed from you. All that is in your possession at present will also leave you (upon your death).

The Fate of Humankind:
Subdue your untamed soul (unrestrained desires of the heart) with the vision (i.e., thought) of death; make it see the transient nature of life and all of its trappings. Let your natural self realize the inevitability of (encountering) misfortunes, adversities, changing circumstances, and changing times. Study the lives of people gone by. See the ruined cities, the dilapidated palaces, the decaying signs, the relics of fallen empires, and the perished nations. Then meditate over the lives of those people, as to what they did when they were alive and were in power, what they accomplished, and what was their contribution to human welfare.

If you carefully ponder over these, you will find that each one of those individuals has parted company with the others, leaving behind all that he cherished and loved, and now he is in a solitary abode (grave). Therefore, (realize that) you will also depart (from this world) in a similar manner.

Take care to provide for your future abode. Do not trade away eternal blessings for the transient pleasures of this mortal world.

Do not talk about things that you do not know. Do not speculate about or pass verdicts on subjects about which you are not in a position to form an opinion, particularly when no one has asked you for an opinion. Give up that pursuit where there is a possibility of your going astray. When there is risk of your wandering in the wilderness of ignorance and the possibility of losing sight of your goal, then it is better for you to give up the quest than to face unforeseen dangers (by losing the straight path).

Defend the Cause of God:
Defend the cause of God. When defending the cause of God, do not be afraid that people will mock you, censure your actions, or even slander you. Help (and defend) the truth and justice fearlessly and boldly. Bear patiently the sufferings encountered and face bravely the obstacles that come your way. Try to be well versed

with jurisprudence and theology, and acquire a thorough knowledge of the canons of the religion.

Your Dealings with Others:
Whatever you like for yourself, the same you like for others; whatever you dislike to happen to you, spare others from such happenings. Do not oppress and tyrannize anyone, because you surely do not like to be oppressed and tyrannized. Be kind and sympathetic to others, as you desire others to treat you. If you notice objectionable and loathsome habits in others, abstain from developing those habits in yourself. If you feel happy and satisfied in receiving a certain kind of treatment from others, then treat others in the same way. Do not speak about others in a way that you do not like others to speak about you. Avoid scandal, libel, and defamation, as you do not like yourself to be scandalized.

Vanity is a Folly that Brings Harm:
Remember, Son, vanity and conceit are a folly. These traits will bring serious harm to you and will endanger your well-being. Therefore, lead a well-balanced life (i.e., neither be conceited nor suffer from inferiority complex) and strive to earn an honest living. Do not be a "treasurer" for others [Note: this is an apt analogy of a miserly person who hoards wealth and dies, leaving behind his wealth to be enjoyed by others]. Whenever you receive guidance from the Lord to achieve a thing you desire, then do not become proud of your blessing, but be humble and submissive to God, realizing that your success was due to His mercy.

Give While You Can:
Remember that your charity and your good deeds are like loans (to God), which He will pay back to you, much in this world, and much more in the Hereafter. Therefore, when you are affluent and have power, make use of your wealth and power in such a way that you will get that returned to you on the Day of Judgment, when you will be needy and helpless. Be it known, My Son, that your passage (from this world to the next world) lies through a dreadful valley, an extremely difficult and arduous journey.

On this journey, a man (traveling) with less weight (i.e., fewer sins and liabilities) is far better than an overburdened person is (with sins and dishonest earnings). The former can travel faster and easier than the latter. You shall have to pass through this valley. The journey will lead you either to Paradise or to Hell. Therefore, it is wise to send your provision beforehand, so that it reaches there (to Paradise) ahead of you. Make advance reservation and arrangements for your stay before you arrive, because after death, there is no possibility of a second chance to make up for the wrongs.

If you find poor and needy persons who are willing to carry your load (i.e., recipients of your disposable wealth given in charity) on your journey to the Day of Judgment, then consider this a blessing. Thus, relieve yourself from the heavy responsibility and liability of submitting an account on the Day of Judgment of how you have made use of God's bounties (i.e., health, wealth, power, and position).

Importance of Self-Respect:

Earn your livelihood through scrupulously honest means and be content with such earnings. Do not let your desires drive you such that you encounter disappointment and loss. Remember that everyone who prays (to God) for a thing will not always get it. One who controls his/her desires safeguards self-respect. At times, you may secure your heart's desires by means that make you lose your self-respect, but nothing in this world can compensate for the loss of self-respect, nobility, and honor.

Take care, My Son, and beware that you do not make yourself a slave (subservient) to another person. God has created you a free man. Do not barter away your freedom in return for anything (of this world). There is no goodness in wealth and power acquired dishonorably.

Greed Leads to Destruction:

Beware, My Son, so that avarice and greed may not drive you towards destruction and damnation. Make nobody but God your benefactor.

Do your best to achieve this nobility, because God will grant you your share (of bounties) whether or not others help you.

To safeguard your possessions and to economize is better than to ask from others. The bitterness of poverty is, in reality, better than the disgrace of begging. Often, an individual tries to acquire a thing that proves to be harmful when gained.

Treat Your Family Well:

Do not ill-treat members of your family, and do not behave with them as if you are "the cruelest person alive." Do not run after a person who tries to avoid you.

The greatest achievement of your character is that, despite the hostility of your brother, you continue to show friendship to him. Do good to your brother, even when he is bent upon doing harm to you. When he ignores or declines to recognize the kinship (with you), attempt to befriend him, help him when he is needy, and try to maintain a relationship. If he acts miserly with you and refuses to help you, be generous with him and support him financially (in his need). If he causes you grief or hurt, be kind and considerate to him in return. If he harms you, accept his excuses. Behave with him as if he is the benefactor and you are the beneficiary.

Be mindful that do not do it inappropriately and when dealing with those who do not deserve.

Treat members of your family with love and respect, because "they are the wings with which you fly and the hands that support and defend you." They are people towards whom you turn when you are in trouble and need help.

Deal with Your Enemy with Consideration:

Be considerate to your enemy, because it will allow you to rise (morally) above him/ her, and/or it will reduce the intensity of his/ her hostility.

If you want to sever relations with your friend, then do not break them off completely, in case you may want to make up with him/ her later.

How to Deal with Oppression:

If you are a victim of oppression, let it not worry you excessively, because an oppressor, in reality, brings harm to himself, and he opens up ways of (spiritual) benefit to you.

Pearls of Wisdom and Guidance to His Son:

- A sensible person pays heed to advice and draws benefit from it. Do not be like a person on whom advice has no effect.
- Beasts are the ones that require coercion for compliance.
- Overcome sorrows, worries, and misfortunes with patience, and with faith in the merciful Lord.
- One who gives up the straight path (forgoes virtue) thereby loses honesty and rational thinking and, as a result, harms himself.
- A true friend is one who speaks well of you behind your back.
- Excessive desires lead to misfortunes.
- Whoever forsakes the truth makes his/her life constrictive and distressed.
- Honesty and contentment are assets that bring prestige and safeguard the status.
- The strongest relationship is the one that is cultivated between God and His subject.
- The person who does not care about you is (akin to) your enemy.
- If there is likelihood of death or harm in pursuing a goal, then safety lies in not pursuing it.
- Do not talk about weaknesses and shortcomings (of others).
- Opportunities do not repeat themselves.
- At times, the wise fail to achieve their goal, whereas the unwise are able to.

- Avoiding ignorant persons is akin to connecting with the wise ones.
- Whoever trusts this world is betrayed, and whoever gives importance to it is disgraced.
- Not every arrow of yours will hit the bull's eye.
- Before buying a house, inquire about the neighbors you will have.
- Avoid ridiculous topics in your conversation, even if you are quoting others.
- Do not let down a person who has a good opinion about you; do not let him change his opinion.
- Do not jeopardize your well-being through irrational, unreasonable, and extravagant hopes.
- Vain hopes are assets of fools.
- Do not be fooled by flattery.
- There are two kinds of livelihood: the one you are pursuing and the other that pursues you. God has the latter destined for you, and it will reach you, even if you do not pursue it.
- Do not befriend the enemy of your friend, lest your friend becomes your enemy.
- Wisdom lies in remembering past experiences and drawing benefit from them.
- The best experience is the one that offers the best advice and teaches caution.
- Take advantage of opportunities before you lose them.
- Not everyone who tries, succeeds.
- No one will return after departing from this world.
- The worst folly is to waste opportunities (to do good) in this life and thereby lose salvation.
- To be submissive and to beg when in need, and to be arrogant and oppressive when affluent and powerful, are two of the ugliest traits of human character.
- Never ill-treat a person who has done you some good.

- Remember, do not overburden yourself with obligations (i.e., do not commit yourself to too many responsibilities), so that you may not be able to fulfil them honorably.

Concluding Remarks in the Letter:

My Dear Son! After having given these pieces of advice to you, I entrust you to the Lord. He will help, guide, and protect you in this world and the Hereafter. I beseech Him to take you under His protection in both the worlds.

JUSTICE, INJUSTICE, AND OPPRESSION

One of the most beautiful names of God is *Al-'Adl*," "The Just." The concept of justice (*'Adl*) is central to the faith of a believer, because God is Just and demands justice from us. Those who practice injustice towards fellow human beings and die unrepentant will carry a heavy burden on the Day of Judgment. Imam Ali (p) practiced the highest standards of justice. He advised his subordinates, the governors, the tax collectors, and the armed forces to uphold the highest standards of justice and showed zero tolerance for unjust behavior. In the following passages, Imam Ali beautifully ties justice together with self-purification, spiritual excellence, and the good pleasure of God.

God is Just to His Subjects:
Certainly, God is not **unjust** to His creatures.
(Sermon 177)

God is Too Exalted to Be Unjust:
He is too exalted to be unjust to His creatures. He deals with equity among His creation and is **just in** His commands.
(Sermon 184)

God's Justice is for Both the Rich and the Poor:
He ordained livelihood with plentitude and with paucity. He distributed it sparingly as well as generously. He did it with justice, to test whomever He desired with prosperity or with destitution, and to test the gratefulness and endurance of the rich as well as the poor. His justice extends to all of them, and His bounty encompasses them despite their shortcomings.

(Sermon 90)

Justice in Distribution of Shares from Public Treasury: When someone asked Imam Ali for an extra share of money from the public treasury,[1] this was his reply: Do you command me that I should oppress those over whom I have been appointed (to administer)? By God, I will not do it, as long as the earth survives, and as long as the stars remain. Even if it were my (personal) property, I would have distributed it equally among them, especially when this property belongs to God. Beware; certainly, the giving of wealth to the undeserving is wastefulness and lavishness. It may elevate the giver (in the eyes of the people) in this world, but it lowers his status in the next world (in the sight of God). It may honor him before the people, but disgraces him before God. If a man gives his property to those who have no right to it, or they do not deserve it, then God deprives him (the giver) of the gratefulness of the recipients. Then, if he (the benefactor) were to fall into hard times and needed help, they (the undeserving recipients) would likely be unworthy comrades and ignoble friends.

(Sermon 125)

Imam Ali's Exhortation to Avoid Vanity, to Take Pride in Being Just, and to Perform Good Deeds:

Your pride should be for acquiring good qualities, praiseworthy acts, and admirable matters.

You should take pride in praiseworthy habits like helping a neighbor, fulfillment of contracts, being with the virtuous, opposing the haughty, extending generosity, avoiding bloodshed, doing justice, controlling anger, and avoidance of making trouble on the earth.

(Sermon 191)

---

1 In those days, funds received from land tax, *Zakaat,* which is obligatory charity, and other incomes to the state were maintained in the public treasury, and then distributed to the needy population.

About the People who Remember (Praise) God, Practice Justice, and Invite Others to Do the Same:
There are some people who are devoted to the remembrance (of God), who have adopted it in preference to worldly matters (material pursuits) so that commerce or trade does not distract them away from God's remembrance. They pass their lives in this manner. They speak to the neglectful persons, warning them against matters held unlawful by God. They enjoin justice, which they themselves practice, and when they forbid the unlawful (and evil) acts, they themselves refrain from them.
(Sermon 220)

His Instructions to His Soldiers Not to Initiate Fighting:
Do not take the initiative in fighting (do not initiate hostilities);[1] let your enemy begin it. It is the Favor of God that you are on the side of truth and justice. Leave them (the enemy) until they begin their hostilities (fighting) and then you are at liberty to fight back. Their (the enemy's) starting the hostilities will be another proof of your obedience to God.
(Letter 14)

His Prayer When Faced with the Enemy:
Lord! Let the truth prevail; let the people realize our **just and** honest stance.
(Letter 15)

His Advice to a Government Official:
If it is possible for you to be sincerely God-conscious and have sincere faith in His Justice, Mercy, and Love (of God), then try to hold firmly the two beliefs (i.e., Heaven and Hell). A man entertains and cherishes the love, reverence, and veneration of God in proportion to His God-consciousness and awe that develops in his mind. Verily, he who fully

1 This was the strict policy of Prophet Muhammad. Imam Ali also adhered to it. Unfortunately, subsequent rulers did not always practice it.

believes in His Justice and fears punishment should expect the best reward in return from God.

(Letter 27)

Part of a Letter Advising His Governors:

Remember: always treat them (your subjects) sympathetically, kindly, courteously, and cheerfully.[1] When dealing them, whether rich or poor, big or small in status, you should behave as if they are your equals, so that important persons of the State may not desire to derive undue advantage out of you, and the poor people may not lose hope in your justice and sympathy....If you give up equity and justice, then you will certainly be considered a tyrant and an oppressor....Remember that nothing can make up for tyranny and oppression.

(Letters 46, 53, 59)

His Advice to the Tax Collectors:

Treat the taxpayers with equity and justice; listen to their needs with patience and kindness, because you are the representative of the people, and the officer representing the authority over you.

(Letter 51)

One of His Sayings:

When Imam Ali (p) was asked about faith, he replied that four pillars support the structure of faith: endurance, conviction, justice, and jihad (struggle):

Justice has four aspects: depth of understanding, profoundness of knowledge, fairness of judgment, and clarity of mind; because whoever tries his best to understand a problem will have to study it, and whoever studies the subject that he is to deal with will develop a clear mind and will come to correct decisions. Whoever tries to achieve all this will have to develop ample patience and forbearance; whoever

---

1 The governor of a province was virtual ruler in those days.

2 Meaning, rich and poor, privileged and underprivileged, of different religious beliefs, etc.

3 For explanation of the term "Saying," please refer to the section of abbreviations.

does this has done justice for the cause of religion, and has led a life of good repute. As far as justice and equity are concerned, your treatment should be fair and unprejudiced to everyone.[2]
(Saying 31)[3]

Injustice and Oppression:
Know that injustice is of three kinds: 1) the injustice that God will not forgive; 2) the injustice that will not be left unquestioned; and, 3) the injustice that may be forgiven without being questioned. The injustice that will not be forgiven is joining other gods with God (polytheism).

God says: *"Verily, God forgives not that (anything) be associated with Him"* (referring to polytheism).
(Qur'an 4:48, 116)

The injustice that will be forgiven is the one that a man does to himself by committing small sins, and the injustice that will be questioned is that done against others. The retribution in such a case may be severe.

O people, blessed is the man whose own shortcomings keep him from (looking into) the shortcomings of others. Blessed is the man who confines himself to his own affairs, eats his (honestly acquired) sustenance, busies himself with obeying God, weeps (in repentance) over his sins, and people are safe (from any mischief) from him.
(Sermon 175)

A Great Injustice:
In a community composed of honest, sober, and virtuous people, forming a bad opinion about one of its members, when nothing unrighteous was actually seen of him, is a great injustice to him.
(A saying)

RIGHTS OF OTHERS

Introduction: Recognizing and fulfilling the rights of others holds a pivotal role in any civilized society. It ensures justice, mutual happiness, and peace. Islam has emphasized rights that are mentioned in the scripture. Moreover, Ali bin Husain, the great grandson of Prophet Muhammad (s), wrote a manual 1,400 years ago known as the "Treatise of Rights." It describes the rights of God over His subjects, the rights of people over God, the rights of parents, children, neighbors, fellow citizens, the ruler, the ruled, etc. About fifty categories of rights have been described.[1] In the following pages, Imam Ali (p) has touched upon some of these rights.

Rights of God Almighty:

O people, remember God, and (remember) that He has enjoined you in His Book (The Qur'an), and His rights that He has entrusted to you. Verily, God has not created you in vain, nor left you free, nor left you by yourself, in ignorance.

(Sermon 85)

Seek assistance of God for fulfillment of His obligatory rights (to testify to His Oneness, not associate anyone else with Him, and to worship Him alone) and (thanking Him) for His countless bounties and obligations.

(Sermon 98)

We praise Him in all His affairs and seek His assistance for fulfillment of His rights.

(Sermon 99)

---

1 See http://www.al-islam.org/sahifa/treatise.html.

To Fulfill the Rights of God:
Seek nearness to God by fulfilling His **rights** that He has enjoined upon you In His Book (The Qur'an). He has clearly stated His demands to you.[2] I am a witness and I shall plead on your behalf on the Day of Judgment.
(Sermon 175)

About Rights of the Subjects:
Nor should he (the ruler) deal unjustly with wealth, thus preferring one group over another, nor should he accept a bribe while making decisions, as he would forfeit the rights (of others).
(Sermon 130)

Fulfilling the Rights of Others:
On whomever God bestows wealth, he should use it in extending goodness to his kinsmen, in pleasing them, in releasing those in chains (of poverty and ignorance), for those suffering from illness, in giving to the poor and to those in debt, and even endure hardship in order to fulfill the rights (of others). Certainly, the achievement of these qualities is the greatest accomplishment in this world, and a means of earning distinction in the next world (the Hereafter), if God so wills.
(Sermon 141)

He (God) has declared paying regard to (the needs of the) believers as the highest of all regards. He has placed their rights in the same grade (of importance) as devotion (to Himself and His Oneness). Therefore, a believer is one from whose tongue and hand every (other) believer is safe, save in the matter of truth. It is not, therefore, lawful to molest a believer, except when it is ordained (by the Law).
(Sermon 166)

---

2 The greatest right of God over humankind is that man should worship Him alone and not associate anything or anyone with Him. Belief in strict monotheism is a key message of God in the scripture Qur'an. God says: "*I have not created the Jinn and humans except that they serve (worship)* Me" (Qur'an 51:56). For an explanation of *Jinn*, please refer to glossary section. Higher form of worship is through knowing God. Serving God is through serving humanity.

Mutual Rights of the Ruler and the Ruled:
The greatest of the rights that God, the Glorified, has made obligatory is the right of the ruler over the ruled and the right of the ruled over the ruler. This is an obligation which God, the Glorified, has placed on each other. He has made it the basis of their (mutual) affection, and an honor for their religion. Consequently, the ruled cannot prosper unless the rulers are sound, while the rulers cannot be sound unless the ruled are steadfast.
(Sermon 215)

Rulers Who Denied the People Their Rights:
Verily, previous rulers have come to a sad end because they denied people their rights; they became corrupted and could be purchased, then succumbed to the temptations of sins and vices, which led them astray, and they followed the wicked.
(Letter 79)

Distribution of Funds (Charity) from Public Treasury:
Woe to the person against whom the poor, the destitute, the beggars, and those who have been deprived of their rights complain before God.
(Letter 26)

Rights of a Friend:
Do not violate the rights of your friend, because when he is deprived of his **rights**, he will no more remain your friend.
(Letter 31)

KINDNESS, COURTESY, GOOD BEHAVIOR TOWARDS KIN

Introduction: The ultimate aim of all goodness is to please God and gain His nearness and not to expect worldly returns. As Imam Ali (p) points out below, any act to please (exclusively) someone other than God is not accepted by God and may not earn reward in the Hereafter. A vain and arrogant person will not get close to God. Kindness and humility are stressed in the Qur'an.[1] It was practiced and taught by Prophet Muhammad (s), so much so that God says in the Qur'an that he was the best example to follow, and that he was an example of "sublime morality."[2] Imam Ali (p) reminds us about the bounties of God, cautions against envy, exhorts his followers to take care of the needs of kin, and reminds us that the first individual who demonstrated arrogance and vanity was Satan.

Verily, the Divine orders descend from Heaven to Earth like drops of rain, bringing to every individual what is destined for him, either plentitude or paucity. Therefore, if you see your comrade with abundant wealth or offspring, you should not feel envious. A believer should

---

1 *"And lower for them (your parents) the wings of humility out of compassion and say: 'Lord, have Mercy on them, as they cherished me when I was little'"* (Qur'an 17:2).

"God does not forbid you regarding those who have not fought you due to your religion, nor drove you out of your homes, if you show them kindness, and be just to them; verily God loves the just ones" (Qur'an 60:7).

2 *" Indeed, there is for you in the Messenger of God (Muhammad) an excellent pattern of conduct, for him who places his hope in God, and the latter day (Day of Judgment), and remembers God much"* (Qur'an 33:21).

"And most certainly you (Muhammad) stand on a sublime standard of morality" (Qur'an 68:4).

not commit such an act that, if it is disclosed, it will make him hang his head low in shame.

A believer who keeps away from the dishonest lifestyle expects one of two good things: a generous livelihood in this life or rewards in the life Hereafter. Wealth and children are the adornments of this world, while virtuous deeds are the source of blessings for the next world. To some individuals, God may grant both of these blessings.

Beware of what God has cautioned you, and be God-conscious so that you may not have to make excuses afterwards. Do not be ostentatious, for if a man acts to please someone else other than God, then God does not accept it.

We ask God (to grant us in the Hereafter) the position of the martyrs (who lay their lives for the sake of God), the company of the virtuous and of the prophets.

O people! Surely no one (even though he may be rich) can do without the help and support of relatives, whether be it physical or moral. They alone are his support, who can ward off troubles and show kindness when tribulations fall. The good memories that a godly man leaves behind among people are better than the property that he leaves behind.

Be careful! If any one of you finds your near relatives in want or starvation, he should not desist from helping them. If one holds back, his hand from (helping) his relatives in need, then at the time of his own need, many hands may remain held back from helping him. One who is sweet tempered in dealing with relatives earns their enduring love (and respect). **(Sermon 23)**

Silence will earn respect and dignity; justice and fair dealings will increase friends; benevolence and charity will enhance prestige and position; courtesy will draw benevolence; service of humanity will enhance leadership; and good words will overcome powerful enemies.

(Saying of Imam Ali)

God Does Not Force Humility:
If God wanted to create Adam from a light whose glare would have dazzled the eyes, whose handsomeness would have amazed the wits, and whose smell would have caught the breath, He could have done so. If He had done so, everyone would have bowed to him in humility, and the trial of Satan and the angels would have been much easier.
(Sermon 191)

Patience and Nobility of Character:
This virtue of patience is one of the highest values of morality, nobility of character, and it is the best behavior that one can adopt.
(Letter 31)

On Politeness:
The best nobility of descent exhibits itself in politeness and in refinement of manners.
(Saying of Imam Ali)

His Advice Regarding Generosity and Good Traits:
You too should take pride in praiseworthy habits, like helping neighbors, the fulfilling of contracts, being with the virtuous, opposing the arrogant, being generous to all.
(Sermon 191)

When one is sure of the returns, he is inclined towards generosity.
(Saying of Imam Ali)

Advice to One of His Governors:
Associate with persons belonging to pious and noble families with high ideals and exalted traditions, families well known for their bravery, courage, generosity, and magnanimity.
(Letter 53)

VIRTUE, ABSTINENCE, AND QUALITIES OF A BELIEVER

Introduction: Moderation in every aspect of life is emphasized in Islam. It was both practiced and preached by Prophet Muhammad (s). Lavishness and asceticism are discouraged. On the other hand, even excessive worship resulting in neglecting one's worldly duties is discouraged.The pursuit of vain desires is a human weakness and a potent weapon of Satan to seduce and misguide. In the following passages, Imam Ali cautions people to stay focused on God in order to avoid Satan's trap.

About Curbing Desires:

O people! Abstinence means to shorten the desires, to show gratitude to God for His bounties, and to keep away from prohibited things. Do not let abstaining from prohibited things make you lose patience (and demeanor). God has exhausted His arguments to you, through clear, shining examples in His manifest books (the Qur'an, the Torah, and the Gospel).

(Sermon 80)

Characteristics of a Believer:

O creatures of God! The most beloved of God is he whom God has given control over his passions. The lamp of guidance is lighted in his heart. He regards what others regard distant (death and resurrection) to be near. He remembers (God) much and strives in His cause. He has a balanced approach to life. He has put off (vain and excessive) desires and is safe from misguidance and passions. He is the key to the doors of guidance and has locked shut the doors of misguidance.

He has held the most reliable and strongest supports. His conviction in God is like that of the brightness of the sun. He has devoted himself to serve God, the Glorified. He is like a lamp (of guidance) in the dark. Everything he did was for the sake of God, so God made him His favorite. He is like a mine of faith (and belief). He has enjoined upon himself (to act with) justice.

The first step of justice for him is the rejection of desires of the heart. He describes what is right and acts according to it. The Qur'an is his guide (in all affairs).
(Sermon 86)

Those Who Walk on the Right Path Are in a Minority:
O people, do not wonder at the small number of those who adhere to the right path. O people, you are grouped (in the sight of God) according to your choice of associating with good or evil. (Recount the story of the people of Thamud in the Scripture ;) only one individual killed the (sacred) camel (in a show of rebellion), but God held all the inhabitants accountable and punished them, because all of them consented to his evil act. They, along with their land, were destroyed. O people, he who treads the clear path (of guidance) reaches the spring of (cool) water, and whoever abandons the right path is like the thirsty traveler who strays into a desert that has no water.
(Sermon 200)

His Advice:
Therefore, man should secure honor by adopting the following qualities: He should fear the Day of Judgment before it arrives; he should realize that the earthly life is short and it is a place of temporary stay. Blessed be he who possesses a virtuous heart, who is obedient to the (righteous) leader and the guide, and dissociates from him who misguides him; therefore, he treads the path of safety (and virtue). By obeying the leader, he hastens towards guidance before its doors are closed and opens the door of repentance and forgiveness, and thereby removes the (stain of) sin.
(Sermon 213)

GOD-CONSCIOUSNESS

Introduction: The Arabic word for God-consciousness is *"Taqwa."* It is actually a comprehensive word with many shades of meaning, including piety, God-consciousness, God-fearing, reverence of God, God-wariness, and fear of disconnecting from God. In the Qur'an, the word *Taqwa* is used more than two hundred times in various situations. All the Prophets (p) of God practiced God-consciousness in its highest form. They taught and guided their followers to God-consciousness. God-consciousness, not wealth or power, brings a person close to God.

Characteristics of a God-Conscious Person:
The admonitions (from God) are effective only on people with pure hearts, listening ears, firm beliefs, and clear minds. One who is God-conscious listens (to good advice), (humbly) accepts it; when having committed sin, admits it; when fearing (the consequence of sin), it causes him to correct his fault; when apprehensive (about the Hereafter), he hastens (towards good acts); and, he performs virtuous acts out of firm belief. When admonished, he pays heed; when asked to abstain (from evil), he complies. He responds to the call (of God) and is drawn (towards Him); when he falls (into evil), he repents; and, when he was shown (the right path), he adopted it.

Such a man was busy in search of truth and got rid (of evils). He collected provision (of good acts), purified his inner self, and collected provision for the next world, being aware of his departure from this world (death); kept in focus his journey (to the next world), and the provisions he will need there. He sent (provision) ahead of himself for the abode of his (permanent) stay (in the Hereafter). O creatures of God, be God-conscious and keep in view the reason for which He has created you. Make yourself deserving of that which He has

promised you (bounties). Have trust in His promises and fear the Day of Judgment.
(Sermon 82)

Enjoining God-Consciousness:
O creatures of God, I advise you to be conscious of God, who has given examples (for your guidance). He has provided clothing to cover yourselves, and He has provided abundant sustenance for you. He has surrounded you with His signs (so that you may know Him). He has bestowed upon you vast bounties and extensive gifts. He has warned you through convincing arguments (against disobeying Him). He has fixed for you a lifespan in this place of trials (the world). You are tested in this world and will give account (on the Day of Judgment).
(Sermon 82)

O creatures of God! I advise you to be God-conscious; it is the provision with which you will return (to the next world). This provision will help you to make your journey to the next world and reach your destination successfully.

O creatures of God! Certainly, God-consciousness saves the God-loving people from unlawful acts. They pass their nights in wakefulness (in prayers), and during the day, they bear thirst (e.g., from fasting for the sake of God). They achieve ease and comfort (in the Hereafter) through bearing hardship and achieve satiation (spiritual) through bearing thirst. They consider death to be near and therefore hasten to perform (good) deeds. They control (unrestrained and vile desires) and keep death in their sight.

The (life of the) world is filled with tribulations, changing fortunes, and (bitter) lessons. It afflicts the living with death, the healthy with ailment, and the one in ease and comfort with distress and calamity.

An Example of Tribulations:
You see a man who collects (wealth) that he may not (fully) make use of, and builds (structures) wherein he may not reside. Then he leaves

(this world) to meet his Lord, but he goes without taking the wealth or the real property with him.

An Example of Changing Fortunes:
You see a contemptible man who becomes enviable and an enviable man who becomes contemptible by losing his wealth and being struck with destitution and misfortune.

As for Its (Bitter) Lessons:
A man is close to achieving his (cherished) desires, and then (suddenly) death strikes; thus, neither the desire is achieved nor the seeker is spared. Glory be to God, how deceitful are the world's pleasures, how insatiable is the thirst for worldly pleasures, and how sunny (hot) is its shade. The approach (of death) cannot be turned back, and the one who departs never returns. Glory be to God, how close death may be to someone, striking (when least expected), and how far removed are the dead (taken to a place of no return).

Nothing is more terrible than evil except its punishment (for the unrepentant), and nothing is more enjoyable than good except its reward. You should know that a little (earned through honest means) is rewarded with much in the next world, and that which is much (earned dishonestly) in this world would earn no reward. In so many cases, little is profitable, while much is a loss.

God has guaranteed your livelihood and has commanded you to act (righteously). Therefore, the pursuit of that which (already) has been guaranteed to you should not get preference over that which has been enjoined upon you (the obligations).

So, hasten towards (good) actions, strive to be pious, and prepare yourself for death (that may approach you unannounced).
(Sermon 113)

Praise be to God, Who made His praise and remembrance a means for the increase of His bounties.

O creatures of God! Time will eventually deal with the living in the same way it dealt with those who passed away. The time gone will not be recovered, and whatever it holds will not remain forever. He who busies himself with something other than reforming himself invites destruction. His base nature immerses him deeply in vices and makes his bad deeds appear (to him) good. Paradise is the destination of those who are forward (in good deeds), and Hell is the abode of those who commit (major) sins (and die unrepentant).

Know, O creatures of God, that God-consciousness is (like) a strong house that gives protection, while impiety is a weak house, which does not protect its people who take refuge therein.

O creatures of God, He has shown you the way of truthfulness and illuminated its paths. Therefore, (you may) choose either misfortune (of pursuing falsehood), or the eternal bliss of the truthful. Collect provision in this life for the Hereafter. Beware the one who was created for the next world; what does he have to do with this world? What will a person do with the wealth that he would shortly leave behind, while carrying only its ill effects (of unlawful hoarding)?

O creatures of God! Do not disregard the good that God has promised to you, and do not covet the evil that He asked you to refrain from. O creatures of God! Be God-conscious and fear the Day when your actions will be judged.

O creatures of God! Your "self" (soul or conscience) is like a guard (watching) over you; your limbs are vigil keepers that preserve (the record of) your deeds, and (even record) the number of your breaths. The gloom of the dark night cannot conceal your deeds from them, nor can you hide even behind closed doors. Surely tomorrow (the Day of Reckoning) is near.

The present will depart with all that it holds, and the future will come in its wake. Everyone will face death and end up in that lonely place,

the grave. Then, (the curtains of) falsehood would be removed from you, and your excuses at that time would be of no consequence. The truth will become evident. All matters related to you would earn their rewards (good or bad). Therefore, take good counsel, learn from examples, and pay heed to warnings.
(Sermon 156)

An Account of People of the Past and Learning from Their Lives:
I advise you, O creatures of God, to practice reverential fear of God (practice God-consciousness), He gave you good clothing and bestowed an abundance of sustenance on you. If there was anyone (in history) who could secure a ladder (to climb up to heaven) to an ever-lasting life, or a way to avoid death, it was Solomon, son of David (p). He was given control over the domain of the Jinn and men, along with bestowal of prophethood and an honored position, but when he finished what was his due in food (end of life of this world) and exhausted his (fixed) time, the bow of destruction shot him with the arrow of death. His houses became vacant and his habitations became empty. Eventually, another group of people inherited them. Certainly, the bygone centuries have a lesson for you.

Where are the Pharaohs? Where are those who advanced with armies, defeated their foes, mobilized forces, and populated the cities?
(Sermon 181)

Importance of Being God-Conscious:
You should, therefore, strive to be God-conscious, because it is a rope that is strong, its height is lofty, and it is indestructible. Be prepared for death before its approach, because the reckoning will be, without doubt, on the Day of Judgment.

"This is a warning for the one with understanding, and a lesson for one who did not know."
(Qur'an 39:73)

They are safe from chastisement and punishment. Their abode will be peaceful and they will be pleased with their lodging. They are the people whose actions in this world were chaste, their eyes were tearful, their nights in this world were like days because of fearing and seeking forgiveness, and their days were like nights because of feelings of loneliness and separation (from their Lord). Therefore, God made Paradise the place of their (eventual) return as a reward and recompense.

Be patient in trials; do not make haste in matters in which God has not asked for haste. Any one of you who dies in his bed while he had knowledge of the rights of God, the rights of His Prophet, and members of the Prophet's house, he will die as a martyr. His reward is incumbent on God and will be eligible to the recompense of what good acts he had intended to do.
(Sermon 189)

Advice to Practice God-consciousness and Caution Against the Love of this World:
I advise you, O creature of God, that you should have God-consciousness, because it is a right of God over you and it creates your right over God, and that you should seek God's help in (achieving) it, and its (God-consciousness') help in (seeking closeness to) God. Certainly, God-consciousness is a protection and a shield, and for tomorrow (the Day of Judgment), it is the road to Paradise. It is a clear path, and whoever treads on it, succeeds. How few will be those who will tread on this path and practice righteousness! They will be very few in number, and they are the people referred to by God Almighty in the scripture as follows:

"And very few of My creatures are grateful!" **(Qur'an 34:13)**

Therefore, hasten towards it (practice God-consciousness) and strive to achieve it. Exchange your sleep (of heedlessness) for wakefulness (of the heedful). Make it (practice God-consciousness) an adornment of your hearts, cleanse your sins with it, and cure your (spiritual) ailments with it. Take a lesson from him (the unfortunate) who neglected it. Beware, you should take care of it and should take care of yourselves through it.

Do not regard him lowly (from his appearance) whom God may have given a high (spiritual) position, and do not consider him high (in spiritual position), simply because this world has given him a high position. Do not cast your eyes on the shining things of the world, do not listen to him who brags about them and beckons you towards them. Its glamour is deceitful, its promises are false, and its wealth is destined to perish.

Beware, this world first attracts (an individual) and then it lets down. It tells lies and misappropriates. It disowns and is ungrateful. It is malicious and abandons (its lovers). It attracts but makes trouble. Its conditions are ever changing, its steps are faltering, its honor is actually disgrace, its seriousness is jest, and its height is lowliness. It is a place of plunder, pillage, ruin, and destruction. About the lovers of the world, the ungodly, the scripture says:

"So wept not on them the heavens and the earth, nor were they respited." ***(Qur'an 44:29)***
(Sermon 190)

God-consciousness is the key to receiving guidance, the provision for the next world, freedom from every type of slavery, and deliverance from ruin. With its help, the seeker hopes to achieve success (salvation).

Perform (good) deeds while high returns are expected, while repentance may be of benefit, while the prayers are heard, and while the conditions are peaceful. Hasten towards (virtuous) actions before old age (makes you feeble), illness incapacitates, or death (overtakes you). Certainly, death will end your joys and pleasures, and it will cause your (worldly) objectives to be unfulfilled. Certainly, it is an unwelcome visitor, but an invincible adversary. It will be as if it came to you all of a sudden.

Therefore, it is up to you to earn the provisions for the life Hereafter. Let not the life of this world deceive you, as it deceived those who came and departed earlier. Their graves became their abodes

and their wealth was inherited by others. They were not aware as to who visited them (at their graves) and they could not even hear those who wept over them. Therefore, beware of this world, which is treacherous, deceitful, and dishonest. Its pleasures are temporary, and the effects from its calamities are lasting.
(Sermon 228)

His Description of a Pious Person:
The God-fearing are the people of distinction. Their speech is to the point, their dress is modest, and their gait is humble. They keep their eyes closed to what God has made unlawful for them, and they tune their ears to the knowledge that is beneficial to them. During times of trial, they remain calm. The greatness of the Creator is in their hearts, and everything else appears insignificant to them. To them, Paradise and its enjoyments are as if they are visualizing them. To them, the sufferings and punishment of Hell are as if they are actually witnessing them.

Their hearts are grieved (from seeing the suffering around them), they protect themselves from evil, their bodies are lean (due to fasting and eating less), their needs are few, and their souls are chaste. They endure (hardship of this life) for a brief period, and they, in return, secure lasting bliss (of the Hereafter). It is a beneficial transaction, and God made it available to them. The world tried to allure them, but they did not respond to it. It laid its snare for them, but they avoided it.

During the nights, they recite the Holy Scripture (the Qur'an), and through its recitation they seek spiritual (uplifting and) purification. When they come across a verse describing Paradise, they are attracted to it and visualize it in their imagination. When they come across a verse which contains descriptions of Hell, they feel as though the sounds of Hell are reaching their ears. They prostrate themselves and beseech God, the Sublime, for their deliverance.

They downplay their good deeds. They are quick to accept blame. When someone praises them, they say to themselves, "I know myself better than others, and my Lord knows me better than I know." They then pray: "O' God, do not deal with me according to what they say, make me better than what they think of me, and forgive me for (those of my shortcomings) which they do not know."

The characteristic of the pious one is that he has strength in religion, he has firmness along with leniency, he has faith with conviction, eagerness in (seeking) knowledge, moderation in riches, devotion in worship, gracefulness in deprivation, endurance in hardship, desire for the lawful, and dislike for greed. He performs virtuous deeds but still feels fear (for not doing enough). He thanks and praises God morning and evening. The coolness of his eye lies in the gifts that are everlasting (in the Hereafter), in preference to the things of this world.

His worldly hopes and aspirations are few and simple, his spirit is contented, his meals are small and simple, his religion safe, and his anger is suppressed. Only good is expected from him. Evil is far removed from him. He forgives him who wrongs him, and he gives to him who deprives him. He behaves well with him who behaves ill with him.

He is soft-spoken; indecent speech is far removed from him. His sins are nonexistent and his virtues are ever many. His manner is dignified during calamities; he is patient in times of distress and is thankful (to God) during times of ease. He deals justly with people, even if he dislikes them, and does not commit sins for the sake of his loved ones. He admits truth, even before evidence is brought against him. He does not withhold what is in his custody and does not forget his obligation. He does not give bad names to others, nor does he harm his neighbor. He does not feel happy at the misfortunes of others; he avoids what is wrong and adheres to what is right.

If he is wronged, he endures and lets God take revenge on his behalf. People feel safe from him. He endures hardships in this life for the sake of the life in the Hereafter. His keeping away from others is by

way of asceticism and purification, and his nearness to those to whom he is near is by way of kindness. His keeping away from people is not by way of vanity or feeling of superiority, nor is his closeness to them just for show.
(Sermon 192)

Benefits to the God-Conscious:

A God-conscious person keeps troubles away from himself; the difficulties become easy for him, the sustenance increases, God's favors pour forth, and blessings descend down like showers. Therefore, be God-conscious. God gives you good advice. He sent His Messenger to preach to you, and He bestows favors upon you. Thus, devote yourselves exclusively to God.
(Sermon 197)

Individuals Whom Neither Merchandise nor Any Sale Diverts from Remembrance of God:

Certainly, God, the Glorified and Sublime, has made His remembrance as a light for the hearts. With the help of this light, the Godly people acquire insight, which guides them to submit to the Divine Will.

During the times when there were no Prophets among people, there were Godly individuals (Saints) through whom God guided His subjects. They gave the good tidings of deliverance to whoever adopted the righteous way, but whoever adopted the wrong ways, they warned him of ruin. In this way, they served as lamps (of guidance) in the midst of darknesses of ignorance.

There are people devoted to remembrance (of God) who have preferred it in place of worldly matters; the commerce or trade does not turn them away from remembrance of God.

You will find them to be fountainheads of guidance. Angels will be circling around them, messages of peace (from heaven) will be descending upon them, and they will be highly honored because God

appreciated their services. They call upon Him with humility, beseeching Him for forgiveness and requesting bounties. God does not become poor by giving, and He does not disappoint those who strive to approach Him.
(Sermon 220)

3. TO CONNECT WITH GOD THROUGH SUPPLICATION

His Supplications

HIS SUPPLICATIONS

Introduction: A supplication, or *Du'aa* in Arabic, is an act of making a request to God and asking for one's need to be filled. In Islam, it holds an important place as a form of worship and a source of achieving nearness and pleasure of God.[1]

Imam Ali (p) taught many supplications. Below are presented a few selected supplications from the book Nahjul Balagha.When recited in the original Arabic language, they have a poetic and rhythmic quality and exert a profound spiritual effect on the reciter as well as the listener.A larger collection of his supplications are available elsewhere.

A Prayer for Rain:

Certainly God tries creatures because of their (unrepentant) evil deeds by decreasing fruits, holding back blessings, and closing the treasures of good, so that he who wishes to repent may repent, he who wishes to turn away (from evil) may do so, he who wishes to recall (forgotten goodness) may recall, and he who wishes to abstain (from evil) may do so. God, the Glorified, has made the seeking of (His) forgiveness a means for the pouring down of livelihood and mercy, as God has said:

"Seek ye the forgiveness of your Lord! Verily, He is the Most-forgiving, He will send (down) upon you the cloud raining in torrents, and help you with wealth and sons (children)." **(Qur'an 17:10–12)**

---

1 God says in the Qur'an: *"And your Lord says, Call upon Me, I will answer you"* (Chapter 40:160).

May God shower mercy on him who turned repentant, gave up sins, and hastened (in performing good acts) before death.

> *"O my God! We have come out to Thee from under the curtains and coverings (of houses) when the children and the beasts are crying, seeking Thy Mercy, hoping for Thy generosity and bounty, and fearing Thy chastisement and retribution. O my God! Give us to drink from Thy rain, and do not disappoint us, nor kill us by years (of drought), nor punish us for what the foolish among us have committed, O Most Merciful of all those who are merciful.*
>
> *My God! We have come out to Thee to complain to Thee, because drought and famine have driven us, distressing wants have made us helpless, and troublesome mishaps have incessantly befallen us. O my God! We beseech Thee not to send us back disappointed, nor to return us with downcast eyes, nor to chastise us (harshly) for our sins, nor deal with us according to our (evil) deeds.*
>
> *O my God! Do pour on us Thy mercy, Thy blessing, Thy sustenance, and Thy pity, and make us enjoy a drink which benefits us, quenches our thirst, produces green herbage with which all that was lost grows again, and all that had withered comes back to life again. It should bring us fresh and plentiful ripe fruits. With it, the plains may be watered, rivers may begin flowing, plants may grow foliage, and prices may come down. Surely You are powerful over whatever You Will."*

(Sermon 142)

A Supplication for Forgiveness:
O my God! Forgive me for what You know about me more than I do. If I return (to the sins), Thou return to forgiveness. My God, forgive me for what I had promised to myself but did not fulfill. My God, forgive me for that with which I sought nearness to Thee with my tongue, but my heart opposed it and I did not perform it. My God, forgive me for

my winking of the eye, the vile utterances, the desires of the heart, and the errors of speech.
(Sermon 77)

His Supplication Praising God and Abasing Himself:
O my God! You deserve handsome description and the highest esteem. If a wish is directed towards You, then You are the best to answer. If hope is invested in You, then You are the Most Honored one from Whom to have hope. My God! Thou hast bestowed on me such power that I do not praise anyone other than Thee, and I do not eulogize anyone save Thee. I do not direct my praise towards others, who are causes of disappointments and misgivings. Thou hast restrained my tongue from praising Your human subjects (in preference to You) and from making eulogies of your creatures (rather than Yours). My God! Everyone who praises, he has the right of (receiving) reward and recompense from the object of praise. Certainly, I have turned to (praising) You with an eye on the treasures of Your Mercy and stores of Your forgiveness.

O my God! Here stands one, who has exclusively believed in Thy Oneness, which is Thy due, and has not regarded anyone deserving of such praises and eulogies except Thee. My want towards Thee is such that nothing except Thy generosity can cure its destitution, nothing can fulfill its need except Thy generosity. So, do grant us (our requests and needs) and make us free from stretching our hands to anyone other than Thee.

"Certainly, Thou art powerful over all things." **(Qur'an 66:8)**
(Sermon 90)

A Prayer Seeking the Protection of God:
Praise be to God, Who made me such that I have not yet met death (I am still alive), nor am I ill, nor have I been called to account for my evil acts, nor am I without progeny, nor have I forsaken my religion, nor do I disbelieve in my Lord. Neither is my intelligence affected, nor have I been punished with the punishment of people of the past. I

am a slave in Your possession; I have been guilty of excesses. You have exhausted Your pleas over me, and I have no plea (before You). I have no power except what You give me, and I cannot evade except what You save me from. O my God! I seek Your protection from becoming destitute despite Your riches, from being misguided despite Your guidance, from being molested in Your realm, and from being humiliated while authority rests with You. O my God! Let my soul be the first of the noble things that You take from me, and let it be the first trust out of Your favors entrusted to me.[1]

O my God! We seek Your protection from turning away from Your command, or revolting against Your religion, or being led away by our desires, instead of (heeding) the guidance that comes from You.
(Sermon 214)

A Supplication Seeking Reliance on God Alone:

O my God! Preserve (thy grace on) my face (my person) with ease in life, and do not disgrace me with destitution, lest I may have to beg livelihood from those who (themselves) receive from Thee, or try to seek the favor from Thy creatures, thereby engaging myself in praising them (instead of Thee). In reality, Thou art the Master, who grants and who withholds (to everyone).

"Verily, You have power over all things." **(Qur'an 66:8)**
(Sermon 223)

Supplication for Guidance and Forgiveness:

O my God! Thou art the most attached to Thy lovers and the most ready to assist those who put their trust in Thee. Thou seest them in their concealments, knowest whatever is in their consciences, and art aware of the extent of their intelligence. Consequently, their secrets

1 The soul is the nonmaterial (metaphysical and immortal) component of human beings, given by God in a pure and pristine form at the inception of worldly life. At death, it will return to God. During its worldly existence, it may stay pure or may be corrupted and abased depending upon the lifestyle, either God-consciousness or sin, respectively. God will judge it and deal according to his Justice and Mercy.

are open to Thee, and their hearts are eager for Thee. If loneliness makes them bored, then Thy remembrance gives them solace. If distresses befall them, they beseech Thy protection, because they know that the reins of affairs are in Thy hands, and that their movements depend upon Thy commands.

O my God! If I am unable to express my request, I am unaware of my needs, then guide me towards my betterment, and guide my heart towards the goal.

O my God! Deal with me according to Thy forgiveness and do not deal with me according to Thy justice. (For Your justice will subject me to retribution.)
(Sermon 225)

4. TO OBTAIN TRUE KNOWLEDGE

His Discourses on Knowledge

HIS DISCOURSES ON KNOWLEDGE

Introduction: Secular knowledge brings recognition and respect to a person and may lead to wealth. Spiritual knowledge helps bring one closer to God. In either case, if the knowledge is acquired and applied, it instills wisdom and refinement, and this is knowledge in the real sense. However, if knowledge does not bring a positive change, then it is merely information. In this chapter, Imam Ali (p) discusses true knowledge with insightful examples.

An Ignorant Scholar:
A scholar who does not act according to his knowledge is like an ignorant person who does not derive any benefit from his ignorance. God will judge a scholar by a higher standard, and he will be held more blameworthy before God (for his/her shortcomings).
(Sermon 109)

About the Duties of an Imam (Leader):
Certainly there is no obligation on the Imam except fulfilling the responsibilities that have been assigned to him by God; namely, to convey warnings, to give good advice, to revive the true teachings of the Prophet, to enforce (religious) law, and to distribute charity to the deserving. Therefore, hasten to acquire knowledge while you are in the proximity of the people of knowledge.
(Sermon 104)

Knowledge of Angels:
(O God) You made the angels reside in the Heavens, high above the earth. They have the most knowledge about You and Your creation.
(Sermon 108)

Knowledge about God:
Praise be to God, Who is such that it is not possible to describe Him or ascertain true knowledge about Him. Since His greatness is beyond the (grasp of) intellect, therefore, intellect (alone) cannot lead to His realm.
(Sermon 154)

Faith Increases Knowledge:
Faith guides towards virtuous deeds, while virtuous deeds help to achieve faith. Faith increases knowledge, and knowledge leads to the remembrance of death (i.e., the inevitable reality).
(Sermon 155)

Knowledge in the Qur'an:
Know that the Qur'an contains knowledge of what is to come about, the stories of the past, the cure for your (moral and spiritual) ills, and regulations to help with whatever (difficulties) you face.
(Sermon 157)

More on Knowledge in the Qur'an:
God, the Glorified, did not counsel anyone (in the past) with the likes of this Qur'an, for it is the strong rope of God and His trustworthy means. It has the blossoming of the hearts and springs of knowledge.
(Sermon 175)

The Qur'an Contains Oceans of Knowledge:
The Qur'an is the gold mine of belief and the source of the oceans of knowledge. It bestows knowledge on him who listens (and pays attention) to it, has worthy parables for him who relates them (to others), and it contains conclusive verdicts for the jurist.
(Sermon 197)

Knowledge about the Rights of God:
Any one of you who dies in his bed while he has knowledge of the rights of God (i.e., obligations to God) and the rights of His Prophet and members of the Prophet's house, his death will be as if he were a martyr. His reward is incumbent upon God.
(Sermon 189)

Satan Seduces the Learned:

O people! Fear the evil consequences of vanity, because vanity is a trap of Satan, and it is his great trick and a poison that enters the hearts of the people. It seldom spares its victim.
(Sermon 191)

Knowledge of the (Chosen) Members of the Family of the Prophet (s):

Know that, certainly, those who are bestowed with God-given knowledge protect what God desires to be protected, and thereby make the springs (of His blessings) flow (for the benefit of humanity).
(Sermon 213)

More about Knowledge of the Family of the Prophet (s):

They are the lifeblood of knowledge and a death knell for ignorance. They comprehended religion in a diligent manner, not acquired by mere hearsay or obtained from relaters, because the relaters of knowledge are many, but those who understand it are few.
(Sermon 237)

The Best Knowledge:

The best knowledge is that which benefits (its possessor).The knowledge which does not benefit (the possessor) is useless and not worth learning.
(Letter 31)

We will be Tested According to Our Knowledge:

Our existence does not end in this world, nor are we (primarily) created for this world.We should not use all our energies to acquire (earthly) pleasures, power, and pomp.We are sent (to this world) to be tested according to the degree of our knowledge (i.e., understanding), our intentions, and actions.
(Letter 55)

Knowledge is a Sign of Distinction:

Knowledge is the best mark of distinction.
(His saying)

Superficial Knowledge:
That knowledge which remains only on your tongue is superficial. The true value of knowledge is realized when you act upon it.
(His Saying)

Advice to Ponder over Knowledge:
Some people show their knowledge by merely talking, while some others ponder upon their knowledge and try to grasp the meaning behind it.
(His Saying)

Thinking Deeply:
No exaltation is superior to knowledge; no knowledge is superior to deep reflection and prudence.
(His Saying)

Knowledge Commands Respect:
Knowledge is power; it commands respect and obedience. A man of knowledge may make people obey and follow him, and after he dies, he is praised and venerated.
(His Saying)

People "Live" by Virtue of Their Knowledge afte Death:
Those who amass wealth, though alive, are dead to the realities of life, and those who achieve knowledge will remain alive by virtue of their knowledge and wisdom, even after they die. The knowledge that they have left behind will remain.
(His Saying)

Knowledge is Power:
Your edge over others is in proportion to your knowledge and wisdom.
(His Saying)

Wisdom and Knowledge:
One who takes lessons from the events of life acquires vision; one who acquires vision becomes wise; and one who attains wisdom achieves knowledge.
(His Saying)

Knowledge is Better than Wealth:

Remember, knowledge is better than wealth, because it guards you, while you have to guard wealth. Wealth decreases if you spend it, but the more you make use of knowledge, the more it increases. What you get through wealth is gone when the wealth is gone, but what you achieve through knowledge will remain even after you are gone. **(His Saying)**

About Knowledge (His Advice to a Companion):

Kumayl bin Ziyad says that once when Imam Ali (p) passed through a cemetery, he heaved a sigh and said:

Kumayl, these hearts (he pointed to himself) are containers of the secrets of knowledge[1] and wisdom, and the best container is the one that holds the most and preserves it (the best). Therefore, remember carefully what I am telling you.

- Remember, there are three kinds of people: the first kind is those learned people who are highly versed in the ethics of truth and philosophy of religion; the second kind is those who are in the process of acquiring knowledge; and the third kind is that class of people who are uneducated (and naive). They follow phony leaders, they believe in every slogan they hear, and they are devoid of rational basis for their convictions.
- Remember, knowledge is better than wealth, because knowledge protects you, while you have to guard wealth. Wealth decreases if you spend it, but the more you make use of knowledge, the more it increases. What you get through wealth is gone when wealth is gone, but what you achieve through knowledge will remain even after you are gone.
- Remember, knowledge is power and it commands obedience. A man of knowledge during his lifetime can make people obey and follow him, and he is praised and venerated after his death.

---

1 The knowledge referred to here is not particularly the secular knowledge of science, math, astronomy, etc. Rather, it is the knowledge about God Almighty, His commandments, His prohibitions, Prophets, His religion, etc.

Remember that knowledge is akin to a ruler, whereas wealth is its subject.

- O Kumayl! Those who amass wealth, though alive, are dead to the realities of life, and those who acquire knowledge will live, by virtue of their knowledge and wisdom, even after their death.

[Kumayl says that after this brief dissertation, Imam Ali (p) pointed towards his chest and said]:

Look, Kumayl! Here I hold treasures of knowledge. I wish I could find someone to share this. A person that I know would sell his salvation in exchange for worldly pleasures; he would make religion a pretense to gain power and wealth, and he would use the blessing of knowledge to control Godly people and exploit unsuspecting individuals. The other person I know had knowledge, but had not achieved the true light of religion, and at the slightest ambiguity or doubt, he would doubt the truth, mistrust the religion, and show skepticism. So, neither of them was capable of acquiring the higher knowledge that is with me.

There is another person who is a slave of his self (i.e., slave to base desires of his soul), and greed easily drags him away from the path of religion. The other person is a miser who will risk his life to grasp and hold on to wealth. Both of these individuals will not be of any use to the religion, nor humanity. They are like beasts, catering to their (biological) needs only. If true trustees of knowledge and wisdom disappear altogether from human societies, then it may bring irreparable harm to humanity. However, this earth will never be without those persons who will safeguard the truth as revealed by God. They may be known individuals who openly expound the knowledge divinely revealed to them, or they may remove themselves from the public gaze due to threat of violence against them. In the latter case, they carry on their mission secretly to preserve and preach the truth as taught by the Prophet of God. I swear by God that these individuals are very few, but their worth and their rank before God is very high. They hand their knowledge and mission to someone like them before they die.

Their knowledge allows them to see the (hidden) realities and the higher truth. Their mission brings excessive hardships on them. They live like ordinary persons, but their souls soar to the heights of Divine Eminence. They are representatives of God on this earth, and they invite people towards Him. How I love to meet them, O Kumayl!
(A Saying)

5. TO AVOID WORLDLY PITFALLS

Worldly Desires, Mixing Right with Wrong

Charity, Misplaced Generosity, Miserliness

About Hypocrisy, Backbiting

WORLDLY DESIRES, MIXING RIGHT WITH WRONG

Introduction: One's heart can be filled with love for worldly things or love for God. It cannot bear both loves at the same time. We are told to enjoy the things of the world but not to covet them. Imam Ali (p) has beautifully stated in the last paragraph of this presentation, "When someone loves a thing, it blinds him and afflicts his heart." Therefore, it is easy to understand that love of this world and its pursuits and pleasures will lead to distancing from God. This will result in corruption of the soul.

Mixing Right with Wrong:
The basic cause of evil is due to pursuit of (worldly) desires. The (vain or excessive) desires and the act of pursuing them are prohibited in the Book of God. If wrong had remained pure, it would not remain hidden, and if right had stayed pure, without admixture with wrong, then those who oppose it would be singled out. However, usually right and wrong are mixed in a manner that people become confused. This is a powerful and effective tool of Satan. Only those who are virtuous and (protected) by God Almighty escape (the clutches of Satan).
(Sermon 50)

Practicing Austerity Will Lighten the Burden in the Hereafter:
Your goal (of reward in the Hereafter) is before you, and the Hour (of Resurrection) is following you. Keep (yourself) light (free of sinful and blameworthy deeds). Those (who have departed earlier) are waiting for you.
(Sermon 21)

About Heart's Desires and High Hopes:

O people, the two things in you that I fear the most are the desires upon which you act and the building of high hopes. Acting upon the desires prevents you from truthfulness, and building of hopes makes you forget the next world (your final destination). Know that this world is advancing rapidly (towards its destruction), and the next world is approaching ever closer. You should pursue the next, not this world, because on the Day of Judgment everyone will be with what he/she pursued. Therefore, this is the time to act, because on the Day of Reckoning it will be too late to repent and get redress.

(Sermon 42)

Love of This World and Its Effects on the Soul:

When someone loves a thing, it blinds him and afflicts the heart. Then he sees, but with afflicted eyes, and hears, but with deaf ears. The desires compromise his intellect, and the (love of the) world makes his heart "dead" (neglectful of remembering God). Consequently, he/she becomes the slave (of the worldly desires) and becomes subservient to anyone who caters those things to him/her and does not take counsel from the preacher, nor pays heed to admonition from God.

(Sermon 108)

CHARITY, MISPLACED GENEROSITY, MISERLINESS

Introduction: The Qur'an has placed great emphasis on charity and generosity. In regards to man's attitude towards amassing wealth, the Qur'an says: "And most surely he is violent in the love of wealth" (100:8). Giving charity both openly and secretly for the good pleasure of God brings one closer to Him. In the following passages, Imam Ali (p) has explained both the benefits and the etiquette of giving charity.

About Charity:
The Islamic charity (*Zakat* or purification) has been laid down (as an obligation). Whoever pays it by way of purifying his spirit, it serves as a purifier for him and a protection and shield against fire (of Hell). No one, therefore, (who pays it) should feel attached to it afterwards, nor should he feel grieved over it. Whoever pays it without the intention of purifying his heart does not receive due rewards. He is certainly ignorant of the teachings of the religion.
(Sermon 198)

About Miserliness:
You do not spend your wealth in God's service, though it is He Who gave you the wealth, nor do you risk (devote) your lives for His sake, though it is He Who created you (and brought you to life). You enjoy honor bestowed upon you by God, the exalted, but you do not honor Him among His creatures. You should derive lessons from your brothers in faith who have departed earlier (from this world).
(Sermon 116)

Misplaced Generosity:
He who shows generosity to those who have no claim to it, or who are undeserving, will not earn anything except the praise of the ignoble and appreciation by the undeserving people, and in the sight of God, the giver might be (considered) a miser.

Therefore, to whomever God gives wealth, he should use it in promoting goodness among his relatives; in entertaining, in helping prisoners and the afflicted; in giving to the poor and to those in debt. He should strive in fulfilling the due rights (of others), endure hardships in the process (if necessary), and thereby expect reward (from God). Certainly, the achievement of these qualities is the height of greatness in this world and the achievement of distinction in the next world (by the Mercy of God).
(Sermon 141)

ABOUT HYPOCRISY, BACKBITING

Introduction: In this chapter, Imam Ali (p) deals with some very important social ills, like hypocrisy and backbiting, which are very detrimental to faith and society. The word "hypocrite" is used in the Qur'an for those individuals who were outwardly Muslim but had hidden enmity toward Islam.[1] They were a liability to the nascent religion of Islam, though people did not know it. On occasions, God would reveal their identities to the Prophet (s), but the Prophet would keep the information to himself and would not expose their hypocrisy. This not only showed the nobility of the Prophet, but also helped keep peace and unity in the community. Backbiting is a major sin in Islam, as is rumor mongering and exposing the sins and shortcomings of others.

Description of Hypocrites:

We praise God for the succor He has given us in carrying out His obedience and in preventing us from disobedience, and we ask Him to complete His favors (on us), and to make us hold on to His rope (support). We stand witness that Muhammad (s) is His servant and His Messenger. He endured every hardship and grief to achieve God's pleasure. His family members and close relatives suffered with him, while the distant relations turned against him. The elders of the community and the population at large declared war against him. People from distant towns and communities united in opposing him.

---

1 "Among people are some who say: 'we believe in God and the Last Day,' (while in fact) they are not believers at all. They intend to deceive God and those who believe, while they (in reality) deceive their own Self (soul), but they do not perceive it" (Qur'an 2:8–9).

I advise you, O creatures of God, to be God-conscious. I warn you of the hypocrites, because they are themselves misguided, and they in turn misguide others. They (pretend to) support you, but they lie in wait to ambush you. Outwardly, they appear friendly and sincere, while their hearts are diseased. They walk stealthily and tread like the approach of sickness (over the body). Their speech is soothing and comforting to the ears, but their intentions and actions are the opposite. Their unsuspecting victims are many. They get your sympathy through cunning and (false) tears.

When they want something, they insist on having it; if they reprove (someone), they disgrace (him); and if they pass a verdict against someone, they commit excess. They find a way to deny or distort every truth. Their speech creates doubts in the mind of the listener. They exaggerate when they describe something. At first, they offer easy solutions, but (later on) they make things difficult. They are the party of Satan.

God says this about hypocrites:

"Satan has gained hold on them, so he makes them forget the remembrance of God; they are Satan's party; beware! Verily, the party of Satan is the loser" **(Qur'an 58:19)**.
(Sermon 193)

About Treason:
O people! Surely, fulfillment of a pledge is the twin of truth. I do not know a better shield (against sin). One who accepts the reality of the return (to God) never betrays. We are in a period when the people regard betrayal as being smart and wise. The ignorant call it cleverness. What is the matter with them? They will face God's wrath and retribution.
(Sermon 41)

About Backbiting and Badmouthing:
Those who do not commit sins and have been safe (from sins) should take pity on the sinners. They keep busy in thanking God and they do not have time for (finding faults of) others. What is the excuse of the backbiter who blames his brother (behind his back) and finds

fault with him? Does he not remember that God has concealed his (the backbiter's) own sins, which were greater than his brother's sins? How can he vilify him (his brother) about his sins when he himself had committed similar sins? Even if he has not committed a similar sin, he may have committed other greater sins. By God, even if he did not commit big sins but committed only small ones, his exposing the sins of others is itself a big sin.

O creature of God, do not be quick in exposing anyone's sin (or faults), for God may already have forgiven him, and do not feel safe in committing even a small sin, because God might punish you for it. Therefore, every one of you who comes to know the faults of others should not expose them, and should keep busy in thanking God that He has saved you from what others have been indulging in.
(Sermon 139)

About Hearsay:
O people! If a person knows his brother to be steadfast in faith and on the right path, he should not lend his ear to what people may say about him. Rumors and loose talk can be far wide of the mark, whereas God is the Hearer and He is the Witness.

"There is nothing between truth and falsehood except four fingers."

Imam Ali was asked the meaning of this statement, whereupon he brought together his four fingers and put them between his ear and eye and said: "It is falsehood when you say, 'I have heard so and so,' while it is the truth when you say, 'I have seen it' (i.e., with one's own eyes)."
(Sermon 140)

6. TO SEEK SOUND ADVICE

His Counsel and Preaching

HIS COUNSEL AND PREACHING, KEYS TO SUCCESS

Introduction: In this collection of admonishment, counsel, and advice, Imam Ali (p) invites people to honesty, truthfulness, and God- consciousness. This demonstrates his superior knowledge and highest level of spirituality. In a few words, he defines success, which is gaining salvation through prayers and thankfulness to God, repentance, and seeking forgiveness coupled with atonement. He is succinct, yet eloquent. The examples and scenarios here are likely to leave a profound impact on the reader.

His Caution about This World:

The Book of God (The Qur'an) is among you, its arguments (are convincing), and its message is firm (and clear). It is like a building whose pillars are strong, and it is indestructible.

God deputed the Prophet (s) after a gap (in time) from the previous prophets, when there was much talk (among the people of his coming). With him, God ended the series of prophets and thereby completed His revelations. He (God) then defended him from those who rejected and opposed him. Those who are "spiritually blind" do not see beyond this (material) world. The sight of a seer (i.e., one who looks with the "eye of the heart") penetrates through and realizes that the (real) abode is beyond this world. The seer, therefore, looks forward to getting out of this world (through inevitable death), while the (spiritually) blind want to stay here (as long as possible). The former collects provision (from this world) for the next world, while the latter collects provision for this world only.

You should know that a human (who is attached to this world) is hardly ever satiated with the life (of this world), because he does not foresee benefit (in the Hereafter) after death.

You team together seeking (worldly) desires and compete fiercely with each other in accumulating wealth. The evil spirit (Satan) has confused you, and his deceit has misled you. I seek the help of God for you and for myself.
(Sermon 132)

His Counsel:
O creatures of God! Derive benefit from preaching and admonition. Your march is towards the place where everyone has to go, namely, death. The scripture says:

"With every person there is a driver and a witness." **(Qur'an 50:21)**

The driver (Angel) leads him towards the day of Resurrection, while the witness (Angel) furnishes evidence about his deeds.
(Sermon 84)

His Admonition:
God's retribution against His enemies is harsh despite His boundless mercy, and His compassion for His friends is great despite His (power of) punishment. He overpowers the one who challenges Him and destroys the one who clashes with Him (e.g., the Pharaoh, who fought against Moses). He disgraces the one who opposes Him and gains sway over one who shows hostility. He is sufficient for the one who puts reliance on Him. He grants him who beseeches Him. He repays the one (generously) who lends Him. He rewards him, who thanks Him.

O creatures of God, examine yourselves (the deeds) before you are examined. Be submissive (to Him) before you are confronted. Know that if one does not become his own counselor (i.e., take charge of his own affairs), then no one else can (do it for him).
(Sermon 89)

Support of the Oppressed:
By God, I will take revenge on behalf of the oppressed and will bring the oppressor to justice.
(Sermon 135)

Advice against Corruption and Oppression:
O people of Arabia, you will be victims of calamities that are very near. You should avoid the intoxication of wealth, fear chastisement that will be in the form of adversities, and keep steadfast in the face of mischief. Beware, the mischief begins imperceptibly, but develops into great hideousness.

Oppressors start (mischief) by (mutual) consultation. They vie with each other in (securing things of) this lowly world. The follower will denounce the leader, and the leader (will dispute with) the follower. They will rebuke and curse one another. The hearts will become wavering (from lack of faith) after being firm, the people will be misled after guidance, the desires will increase, and opinions will become contradictory.

Whoever advances towards this mischief will be ruined, sound judgment will be scarce, and the oppressors will be outspoken. This mischief will shake the pillars of faith and shatter the ties of firm belief. The wise will keep away from it, while the wicked will embrace it. It will create chaos. People will forsake kinship and will abandon faith.

Some (honest) people will be killed and become martyrs, and some others will be fear-stricken, (desperately) seeking protection. People will be deceived by phony pledges and fraudulent belief. At that time, you should not become party to mischief and innovations; instead, become the pillars of obedience (to God). Proceed towards meeting with God as one oppressed, rather than as an oppressor. Avoid the paths of Satan and the places that are plotting revolt. Do not fill your bellies with unlawful morsels. You will (ultimately) meet God, Who has made His obedience easy for you, and has declared disobedience unlawful.
(Sermon 150)

His Advice Against Heedlessness:

God will make clear to the (unrepentant) sinners the punishment for their sins and remove the veils of their heedlessness. I warn you and myself from such a fate. A prudent individual listens, ponders, observes, and derives benefit from good counsel. He treads on a clear path and avoids pitfalls.

O my listeners! Come out of lethargy, wake up from slumber, and check your hasty actions. Ponder over what has come to you through the Prophet, i.e., the inevitable (the Day of Judgment). Do away with your vanity, drop your haughtiness, and recall your final place of rest (i.e., the grave). You will be dealt with as you deal with others, you will reap what you sow, and what you send today will confront you tomorrow. So provide for your day (of reckoning). Fear, O listeners! Act now, O careless! No one will warn you like him who is bestowed with knowledge (from God).

If a person leaves this world to meet God with one of the following acts unrepentant, then his good deeds will not save him from punishment:

a) Associated a partner with God
b) Willfully killed an innocent human being
c) Broadcast the faults and sins of others
d) Introduced innovation in religion for personal benefit
e) Dealt with people with a double face
f) Engaged in double-dealings

(Sermon 152)

Fate of an Oppressive Leader:

I advise you to be God-conscious. You should know that among all the creation, the most distinguished person before God is a just Imam (leader) who is (divinely) guided and he, in turn, guides others. He stands by the recognized ways of the Prophet's teachings and opposes innovations (in religion). Certainly, the worst person before God is an oppressive Imam (leader) who went astray, and thereby misguided others.

(Sermon 163)

Fulfilling the Rights of Others:

God, the Glorified, has sent down a guiding Book (the Qur'an), wherein He has explained virtue and vice. You should adopt virtue, whereby you will receive guidance, and keep away from vice, so that you walk on the right path. Fulfill your obligations for the sake of God, and it will lead you to Paradise. Surely God has made certain things unlawful, and He has declared certain things lawful. He has declared paying respect to fellow believers to be highly important. He has placed their rights in the same degree (of importance) as devotion (to Himself). Therefore, a believer is one from whose tongue and hand every (other)believer is safe. Thus, it is unlawful to oppress or harass a believer.

Be God-conscious in the matter of (the rights of) His creatures and His cities, because you will be questioned even about the land and the beasts (i.e., environment and ecosystem). Obey God. When you see virtue, adopt it, and when you see vice, avoid it.

(Sermon 166)

Caution against the Deception of this World:

O creatures of God! I advise you to be God-conscious, because it is the best advice and the best of all things in the sight of God. You should carry out your duties and desist from the prohibited (acts). Do not make haste in (acting upon) a matter until you have ascertained its correctness.

Know that this world, which you covet, sometimes upsets you and sometimes pleases; it is not your (permanent) abode, nor the place of your stay for which you were created. Know that it will not last forever, nor will you live here indefinitely. While you are here, advance towards that house to which you have been called (in the Hereafter) and your hearts turn away from (love of) this world.

(Sermon 172)

His Advice to Be Obedient to God:

Obey the commandments of God, because God has provided you clear guidance and you have no excuse (to act otherwise). He has clearly explained to you the acts He approves and the acts He disapproves. The Prophet of God used to say: "*(The Road to) Paradise is surrounded by unpleasant things* (i.e., duties, trials, and tribulations), *while* (the Road to) *Hell is surrounded by* (alluring) *desires.*"

You should know that obedience to God might appear to be unpleasant (sometimes), while His disobedience may seem enjoyable (often). May God have mercy on the person who controlled his desires and curbed (vain) appetites of his heart, because the heart leads to disobedience through desires.

O creatures of God, know that this Qur'an is a counselor and a guide that never deceives or misleads and does not contain any falsehood. No one will read or listen to this Qur'an but that his guidance will increase, or a certain (spiritual) blindness will be removed. Therefore, seek cure for your ailments from it and seek its help in (overcoming) your distresses (and difficulties). It cures many spiritual ailments, like unbelief, hypocrisy, misguidance, etc. Therefore, seek approach to God through it (the recitation of the Qur'an) and through prayers.
(Sermon 175)

About Verbal Abuse of One's Enemies:
I dislike you badmouthing (even) your enemies. However, if you recollect and recount their actions, that would be better. Instead of abusing them, say, "O God! Save our blood and their blood, produce reconciliation between them and us, and lead them out of their misguidance, so that he who is ignorant of the truth may acquire knowledge of it, and he who inclines towards rebellion may turn away from it."
(Sermon 205)

About Self-Deception, Neglect, and Ignorance:
O people! What has emboldened you to (commit) sin? What has deceived you about God and made you content with self-destruction? Is there no cure for your ailment or no awakening from your sleep (of heedlessness)? Do you not take pity on yourself, as you do on others? Generally, when you see anyone exposed to hot sunlight, you

provide him with shade, or if you see anyone afflicted with severe pain, you weep (show compassion) out of pity for him. What has made you so tolerant about your own (spiritual) affliction? What has prevented you from weeping over yourselves, although your life is the most precious of all lives to you, and why does not the fear of an ailment that may befall you at night keep you wakeful, although you are on the way to the wrath of God because of your sins?

You should strive to get rid of the ailment that has afflicted your heart, and wake up from the sleep of the heedless. Strive to be obedient to God and love (enjoy) remembering Him. You are running away from Him, while He is calling you to Himself. He is calling you to forgive and cover your faults out of His kindness. Certainly exalted is God Almighty, Who is generous, whereas you are weak (in faith), yet so bold to disobey Him, knowing that you live under His protection and your nourishment comes from His unlimited kindness. He does not deprive you of His kindness and does not remove His protection. In fact, you have not been without His kindnesses even for a single moment, a favor that He conferred, a sin that He concealed, or a calamity that He warded off!

Truly, the world did not deceive you, but you chose to be deceived by it. It is a fair abode for him who is not attached to it and an agreeable place for him who does not regard it as a permanent abode.

Only those who reject (attachment to) this world will be regarded as virtuous in the Hereafter. When the earthquake will shake the earth and the Day of Resurrection is heralded with all its severities, then the people will seek refuge in the places of their worship. They will cling to the object of their devotion. People will be in groups with their respective leaders. On that Day, arguments will prove useless and excuses will be rejected.

Therefore, you should now adopt for yourself the course with which your excuse may hold good and your plea may be accepted. From the things of this world, take those that will be of use to you (in the next

world), gather provisions for your (eternal) journey, and keep (your) sight on the deliverance (in the Hereafter).
(Sermon 221)

A Man in the Audience Requested Imam Ali to Preach about Leading a Sober Life:

Imam Ali thereupon advised him thus:

Do not be among those people who want to gain good returns without working for them, or those who have big hopes and keep on postponing repentance and penance, and who talk like the pious but prefer worldly pleasures.

Do not be among those who are dissatisfied despite being bountiful; they are not content with their modest means. They do not thank God for what they receive and keep on asking for more. They invite others to good deeds that they themselves do not practice; they appreciate goodness in other people, but do not adopt it; they dislike evil and vicious people, but actually they follow their ways of life. They are afraid of death because of their numerous sins, but do not amend their sinful lifestyle. If fallen ill, they show repentance, but on regaining health they fall back into their old ways; when faced with misfortune, they turn to God, beseeching Him for relief, and when relief comes, they are deluded by their ease and comfort and become heedless, and they forsake (mandatory ritual) prayers.

Their minds are allured by daydreaming and high hopes, and they abhor facing the realities of life; they predict severe punishment for the sins of others, but for their own sins they expect very light chastisement. Riches make such people arrogant, rebellious, and wicked; and financial difficulty makes them despondent and dejected.

Calamities and adversities make them lose hope, and they become impatient. They are good at preaching but poor in implementing. They are quick to acquire temporal pleasures but are careless about earning benefits of the Hereafter. They often censure others, being quick to

pass verdicts, and are boastful of their own deeds while they overlook their own faults. They prefer the company of the rich and influential, wasting time in luxuries and vices, and they are averse to the company of the less privileged, pious people. They demand obedience from others, but they are not obedient to God. They collect their dues readily, but do not readily give up that which belongs to others. They do not fear God; they fear His subjects instead.
(Letter 31)

His Advice (Will) to His Sons:

(This advice was given before his death, after an enemy fatally injured Imam Ali on the head with a poisoned blade while he was praying in the mosque.[1])

My sons, I advise you to be God-conscious. Do not go after this corrupt world, though it may try to entice you. Do not seek it, though it may seek you, and do not grieve over and yearn for things that this world denies you. Let the eternal reward and blessings of God guide you for all that you say and do. Despise tyrants and oppressors and be a friend and helper for the oppressed.

To you, and to my other children, and to my relatives, and to all who receive a will of mine, I enjoin you to be God-conscious and to be pious; to do fair and honest dealings with one another; and to strengthen bonds with your kin, because I have heard your grandfather, the Prophet (s), saying: *"To remove mutual enmity, ill feeling, and hatred is better than (optional) prayers and fasting."*

Be God-wary when the helpless orphans are the issue. You should never let them starve. As long as you are there to guard and protect them, no harm should come to them. The Prophet (s) had always advised, cautioned, and reminded us of this responsibility, so much so

---

1 Ali (p) survived for three days after the injuries. He continued to advise and preach, and made his last will and testament.

that we often wondered that the Prophet of God might even assign the (orphans) a share from our inheritance.

Be God-wary regarding what is in the Holy Qur'an, lest others should surpass you in following its tenets and obeying its commands. Fear God in regards to keeping up with (obligatory) prayers, because (obligatory) prayers are pillars of your faith. Be God-wary in regard to His Holy House (K'aba). Let it not be deserted, because if it is deserted, then you will be the losers. Do not be forgetful of God. Struggle in His cause with your tongue, with your wealth, and with your lives. Develop mutual friendships, love, and support for one another. Take care that you do not spurn and treat one another in an uncaring and unsympathetic manner. Exhort people to do good and enjoin them to abstain from evil. If you do not, then the vicious and the wicked will become your rulers, and if you willingly allow them to be your rulers, then God will not answer your prayers. O people, let there be no (acts of) revenge against my murderer, and do not roam about with drawn swords. Moreover, do not start a massacre of my opponents and enemies.

See to it that only my assassin alone is executed as punishment (according to the law of the land), for the punishment of the crime of murder is death for the murderer, and nobody else should be molested.

The execution of the man who injured me shall take place only when I succumb to the wound delivered by him, and this punishment shall be only one stroke of the sword to end his life. He should not be tortured before his death, and his hands and feet should not be amputated, because I have heard the Prophet (s) saying: *"Do not mutilate anyone, be it a vicious dog."*
(Letter 47)

The Wonderful Human Brain

Look at the brain of a human being; it is a wonderful organ. Look what good and bad tendencies originate from it. On one hand, it holds

treasures of knowledge and wisdom, and on the other hand, it harbors lowly desires. If a man gives way to avarice, then excessive desires ruin him. If he is disappointed, then he is overcome with despondency. If he gets agitated, he loses temper. If he is pleased, then he gives up precaution. Sudden fear makes him stunned and nervous, and he is unable to think and find a way out of the situation. During times of peace and prosperity, he becomes careless and unmindful of the future. If he acquires wealth, then he becomes haughty and arrogant. If he is plunged in distress, then his agitation, impatience, and nervousness disgrace him. If he is overtaken by poverty, he finds himself in a very sad plight. Hunger makes him weak and overeating harms him. In short, every kind of loss and gain makes him mentally (and emotionally) unstable.
(Saying of Imam Ali)

The World is a Place to Earn Rewards in the afterlife:
Certainly, this world is a house of truth for those who look into it carefully. It is an abode of peace and rest for those who understand its ways and moods, and it is the best working place for those who want to earn rewards for life in the Hereafter. It is a place of acquiring knowledge and wisdom for the seeker and a place of worship for the friends of God. It is the place where Prophets received revelations from God. It is the place for virtuous people and saints to perform good deeds and to earn rewards. Only in this world could they earn God's favors, rewards, and blessings by performing good deeds. Where else could all these be accomplished? It has taught us that all of its inhabitants are to face death (eventually). It has given an indication of calamities that may befall, and its pleasures are short-lived. It raises hope of prosperity in the evening and causes anxieties and worries the next morning. There are people who will praise this world on the Day of Judgment for reminding them of the Hereafter, for they benefited in the afterlife from their works (in the worldly life).
(Saying of Imam Ali)

Keys to Success:
Possessing the following four qualities are keys to benefit and success:

1. One who prays to God and beseeches Him will not be deprived of the answer to his/her prayers.
2. One who repents (sincerely) will not be denied acceptance of the repentance.
3. One who atones for his/her sins will not be deprived of the salvation.
4. One who shows gratitude to God for blessings and bounties will not be denied the continuation (of blessings) and may receive an increase in the bounties.

God grants the request of one who asks him, grants forgiveness to one who repents, and He will increase the bounties and blessings for one who shows gratitude to Him.
(A Saying)

Advice to His Son:

My son, learn four things from me, and through them you will learn four more. If you keep them in mind, your actions will not bring any harm to you.

1. The greatest wealth is wisdom.
2. The greatest poverty is stupidity.
3. The worst antisocial traits are vanity and self-glorification.
4. The best nobility of descent exhibits itself in politeness and in refinement of manners.

The next four things, my son, are:

1. Do not make friendship with a foolish person, because when he tries to do you good, he will actually do you harm.
2. Do not make a miser your friend, because he will run away from you at the time of your dire need.
3. Do not be friendly with a vicious and wicked person, because he will sell you and your friendship at the cheapest price.
4. Do not befriend a liar, because, like a mirage, he will make you see things near which in reality are very far, and vice versa.

His Advice to His Uncle:

Sometimes a man feels happy for obtaining a thing, being unaware that it would have come to him in any case because it was so destined. Sometimes a man becomes sad at not being able to obtain a (certain) thing, being unaware that it was not destined for him and he could never have acquired it. The things that should please you are the ones that will bring you reward in the Hereafter, whereas you should feel sorry only for losing the rewards of the next world.

(Letter 22)

7. TO GOVERN JUSTLY

Letter to Maalik-al-Ashtar, the New Governor of Egypt

Advice to Governors and Public Officials

His Instructions to Army Officers

His Fiscal Policies, Instructions to Tax Collectors

LETTER TO MAALIK-AL-ASHTAR, THE NEW GOVERNOR OF EGYPT

Due to its excellence, this letter was read in the United Nations by the secretary general

Introduction: This letter contains orders issued by Imam Ali (p) to Maalik- al-Ashtar, the newly appointed governor of Egypt. The governor's duties included collecting religious tax, combating the enemy, looking after the welfare of the people, and ensuring the region's prosperity. The principles laid down in this letter are profound, unique, and of far-reaching significance. These principles of governing in a just and honest manner are so outstanding that this letter was read in an economic forum in the United Nations by the then Secretary General as guidelines for world leaders.

In the name of God, the Beneficent, the Merciful, I order you, O Maalik, to be God-conscious at all times, to give priority to worshipping Him, and to obey His Commands in preference to everything else in life, to obey the commandments faithfully according to the Holy Scripture, as well as the teachings of the Prophet (s). The success of a person to achieve happiness in this world and in the next world depends on it.

I order you to use all your faculties and limbs to help your subjects (the creatures of God), because Almighty God helps those who sincerely try to help Him (through helping people). God has further ordered you to keep your desires under control and to restrain yourself against vice and wickedness. Your soul (base self) incites and drags you towards infamy and damnation, unless the Merciful Lord comes to your help (to guide).

This is only a portion of the lengthy document. For reading the full document, please refer to the original text in English at www.nahjulbalagha.com

Let it be known to you, that I am sending you as the governor to the country that has seen many regime changes. Some of them were benign, sympathetic, and good, while others were tyrannical, oppressive, and cruel. People will judge your administration in the same manner as you have done to other regimes.

You must know that a good and virtuous person is recognized by the words of approval by others. Therefore, make yourself a fountainhead of goodness in thoughts, intentions, and deeds. This can only be achieved by controlling desires, regardless of how strong they are. Remember that the best way to do justice to your inner self and to keep it out of harm's way is to exercise restraint from falling victim to vice and (base) desires.

You must create in your mind kindness, compassion, and love for your subjects. Do not behave towards them as if you are a ravenous beast and as if your success lies in devouring them.

Use Mercy and Compassion in Dealing with Your Subjects: Remember, your subjects are of two categories: Either brothers of yours in faith, or peers of yours in humanity. People of either category suffer from the same weaknesses and defects that human beings are inclined to; they commit sins, indulge in vices, either intentionally or unintentionally, not realizing the enormity of their deeds. Let your mercy and compassion come to their rescue in the same way that you expect God to show you mercy and forgiveness. You must never forget that you are a ruler over them, the Caliph is the ruler over you, and God is the Supreme Lord over the Caliph. The truth is that God has appointed you as the governor to test you by giving you authority over people.

A false sense of prestige is akin to declaring war against God. You can never free yourself from the need of God's Mercy and Compassion.

Do not hesitate to forgive and forget. Do not be too quick to punish, and do not be proud of your powers. Do not get easily angered, and do not lose your temper over the mistakes and failures of your subordinates. Be patient and be sympathetic. Anger or desire of vengeance will not help you. Never tell yourself, "I am their Lord, their ruler, and I must be obeyed submissively and humbly," because such a thought will make you vain and arrogant, and it will weaken your faith in God. If you take pride or feel vain because of your authority, then think of the supreme authority and rule of the Lord of the Universe. Think of the vastness of His creation, His Might, His Glory, His absolute Power to do whatever He wills, which you cannot even dream of possessing. Such thoughts will keep you away from vanity, arrogance, and haughtiness, and it will restore sanity and balance in your mind.

Oppression Invokes God's Wrath:

Never pretend to possess power and might similar to that of God's, because the Mighty Lord will always humiliate and degrade tyrants. As far as your personal affairs (including relatives and friends) are concerned, make sure that they do not conflict with the duties of your office laid down upon you by God, and that you do not usurp the rights of the people. Be impartial and be just to them, because if you give up equity and justice, then you will certainly become a tyrant and an oppressor. Whoever oppresses the subjects of God will earn His wrath and the hatred of those oppressed; and whoever earns the wrath of God, he loses the chances of attaining salvation. He will not have an excuse to offer on the Day of Judgment.

Every tyrant and oppressor is an enemy of God, unless he repents and reforms. Remember, there is nothing in this world more likely to turn God's Blessings into His wrath than to persist upon oppressing His subjects, because the Merciful God always hears the prayers of the oppressed. You must adopt a policy that is neither too severe nor too lenient, a policy that is based upon equity. Remember that the dissatisfaction of common folks and the have-nots weighs heavier than the approval of a few important persons. The displeasure of a few important people will be excused by the Lord if the masses are happy with you.

The poor and Less Privileged are Strong in Faith:

Remember! The "big and important" persons are (quite often) mentally the scum of the human society. They will be a drag upon you during your moments of peace and happiness, and they will be least useful to you during your hours of need. They hate justice the most, will keep on demanding from you more and more of the State's resources, and will seldom be satisfied with what they receive. They will not feel obliged for the many favors received, if any of their unjustified demands are rejected; they will never accept any reasonable excuse or any rational argument. You will not find them faithful and loyal.

The common folks, the poor, and the less privileged among your subjects are the pillars of the religion. They are the real power and defense against the enemies of the state. Pay due attention to their affairs, be friendly with them, and gain their trust and goodwill. Do not pry into shortcomings in people that are not obvious. Leave them to God. However, those weaknesses in your subjects that come to your attention, you must help them to overcome those weaknesses. Do not expose the shortcomings of the people, so that God may conceal yours.

Discourage envy among the people and try to root out mutual distrust and enmity among your subjects.

Deal with All using Justice:

Be fair and just in your dealings with all, and be careful not to make your personality, position, and actions as a source of malice. Do not let any undeserving person get too close to you. Never lower your dignity and prestige. Remember that backbiters and scandalmongers belong to a mean and cunning group, though they pretend to be sincere advisers. Do not make haste to believe in the news they bring and do not pay (much) heed to their advice.

Do not accept the advice of miserly people; they will try to keep you away from acts of kindness and good deeds. They will try to make you fear poverty.

Similarly, do not let cowards act as your advisers, because they will make you timid in enforcing your orders, scare you from courageously handling important affairs, and make you less effective. At the same time, avoid a greedy and covetous person who would aspire to the position of acting as your counselor and advise you to exploit the community and oppress the people. Remember that miserliness, cowardice, and greed arise from lack of faith and trust in God.

The worst among your officers will be the ones who had served under despotic rulers and had committed atrocities. Find individuals who are wise, learned, honest, truthful, and pious. Such individuals will prove the least troublesome to you. They will be sympathetic to your causes. Keep such people with you as your companions and take them to official public meetings. Some of them would receive your full confidence and trust. They are those who can always speak out the truth without reservation, without fear of your status, and would refuse to cooperate with you in any action that God may not approve. Train them not to flatter you and not to seek your favor by false praises, because flattery and false praises create vanity and conceit.

You should not treat good and bad people alike, because in this way you will be discouraging good persons and emboldening the wicked. Everyone should be treated according to what he/she deserves.

Realize that a ruler can create goodwill, faithfulness, and sincerity in the minds of his subjects only when he is kind and considerate to them when addressing their needs and does not oppress and demand from them what is beyond their means. These are the principles that you should keep in mind, and you must act upon them. Let your attitude be such that people do not lose faith in you, because good faith on their part will reduce many troubles of your administration and will relieve you of many worries and anxieties. Put your confidence and trust in those whom you have tested. Do not give up those practices which have created unity and amity among the various sections of the society and which have benefited the masses. Do not break them and do not introduce innovations, because if you do away with the good rules and traditions, the divine punishment of having despoiled them will be your lot.

Different Classes of People in the Society:

You must know that the people over whom you rule are divided into various classes. The prosperity and welfare of the classes of the society is interdependent upon their mutual well-being, such that the whole setup is like a closely woven net. One class cannot exist peacefully, happily, and cannot function without the support and the goodwill of the other.

There is the class of soldiers who defend (the state for) God's cause. The next class is that of the secretaries and the clerks. The third is that of the judges and magistrates. The fourth is that of the officers who maintain law and order. Then there are common folks, the taxpayers. Next is the class of men who are professionals and merchants, and the last, but not the least, are the poor and the have-nots, who are at the lowest segment of the society. The Merciful God has fixed rights and duties for each one of them, a complete code that is with us.

- As far as the soldiers are concerned, they guard and defend the State and its inhabitants. They maintain peace. In fact, they are the real guardians of peace, and they help maintain a sound administration. The upkeep and maintenance of an army depends upon the taxes collected by the State. Out of that, God has fixed a share for them.
- The common folks constitute an important class of citizens, but in a Welfare State their well-being cannot be guaranteed without proper functioning of the other classes, including the judges and magistrates, the secretaries, and the officers of various departments who collect revenues, maintain law and order, as well as preserve peace and amity among the various classes of the society.
- The prosperity of the society depends upon the traders and industrialists. They act as a medium between the consumers and the suppliers. They know the needs of the society. They provide

consumer goods, the essential necessities of life, and operate markets and trading posts.

- ❖ Then next is the class of the poor, disadvantaged, and the disabled. It is absolutely necessary that they should be looked after and adequately provided for. The Merciful God has described the ways and means of providing for this class. Every member of this class has the right, upon the ruler of the State, to receive help for their basic needs.

Remember that Almighty God will not absolve any ruler from his obligations unless he sincerely tries his best to discharge them. Therefore, invoke God to help you in the discharge of your duties you encounter.

Choosing the Commander-in-Chief of the Army:

He should be a person who is most sincere and faithful to God, to the Prophet (s), and to the Imam (spiritual leader). The candidate should be one who is pious, known for his forbearance, clemency, and gentleness, who is neither short-tempered nor does he get angry quickly, who sympathetically evaluates just excuses and accepts apologies; who is kind and compassionate with the weak, but severe against the strong and the powerful; who has no vindictiveness that might lead to (in his subjects) violence or an inferiority complex, or weak-mindedness, or that makes people feel helpless and dejected. To find and select such a person, you should make contacts with honorable and noble families well known for their bravery, courage, generosity, and magnanimity.

When you have found and selected such a person, then keep an eye on him, as a parent watches over the child, so that you discover if there appears any change in his behavior. Treat him kindly. Do not deny deserving promotions or small requests. This will make him trust you, and he will be faithful to you. Do not overlook his minor needs, because small favors often yield good results. Paying careful attention to his major needs is very important.

His Concluding Advice:

Imam Ali (p) here enumerates what is required of a ruler. For the sake of brevity, only pointers are given here. For the interested reader, the details are available elsewhere.

- Do not keep secluded from people for an extended period.
- Neither be overly generous, nor be stingy.
- Watch out for your favorites, who may want to take advantage of you.
- Give due rights to whomever they may belong.
- Make peace with your enemy at every opportunity available.
- Honor pledges and agreements made with the enemy.
- Avoid shedding blood without justification.
- Avoid conceit and self-admiration.
- Avoid laying obligation on your subjects for helping them as part of your job.
- Do not appropriate a share for yourself more than what is due.

His Concluding Remarks:

I pray to God invoking His limitless Mercy and His Might, that He incline us towards goodness, and to guide you and me to that which will please Him and will earn pleasure of the people and bring prosperity and honor. May He cause you and me to die as martyrs (in His service). In the end, we all return to Him. I end the message by sending peace and blessings on the Prophet and his purified descendants.

ADVICE TO GOVERNORS AND PUBLIC OFFICIALS

Introduction: In this chapter, Imam Ali (p) deals with the responsibilities and methods of administration for government officials under his rule. He places the highest emphasis on honesty, integrity, observing the law, humility, and charity. Above all, he emphasizes awareness of accountability to God for the actions of an administrator or a high government official.

Mutual Rights of the Ruler[1] and the Subjects:

God, the Glorified, by placing me over your affairs, has given me a right over you, and similarly you have a right over me. A right may be very vast in description, but very precise in its application. A right also carries accountability to the same degree. God, the Glorified, has decreed (as) His right that His subjects should worship Him alone, and has made incumbent upon Himself to reward them abundantly. He created certain rights for some people against others. Some of these rights give rise to other rights.

The greatest of rights that God, the Glorified, has made obligatory are the rights of the ruler over the ruled, and the rights of the ruled over the ruler. The subjects cannot prosper unless the ruler is sound, while the ruler cannot be sound unless the subjects are steadfast. If the subjects fulfill the rights of the ruler and vice versa, then the religion is correctly practiced, and justice is established. This will lead to a stable government and will discourage the foes. However, if mutual rights are not upheld, then it will lead to oppression and mischief in the land. The desires would be aroused, the commands (of religion) would be dis-

---

1 This term signifies high governing official(s) wielding authority.

carded, diseases of the soul would increase, and greater wrongs would be committed. In such circumstances, the virtuous are humiliated while the vicious are honored. The chastisements from God, the Glorified, will then come upon the people.

You should therefore counsel and cooperate with one another (for the fulfillment of your obligations). This is an obligation on all people from God, regardless of their position, honor, and God-consciousness.

If a man regards God's glory to be supreme, then he should regard everything else to be less significant. God's bounties do not increase without a reciprocal increase in God's right over His subjects.

The worst traits in a ruler are vanity and pride. I abhor high praises accorded to me. God, the Glorified, is more deserving of such praises. Do not praise me for the obligations I discharge, because I fear about those obligations which I have yet to discharge, and do not address me in a manner that (fearsome) despots are addressed. Do not show flattery to me and do not think that I will be offended when a truth about the affairs of state is pointed out. Therefore, do not hesitate in pointing out a matter of justice, because I do not regard myself above committing an error. Certainly you and I are servants of God; there is no lord except Him. He is the owner of our souls. He bestowed upon us prosperity, guidance, and intellect.
(Sermon 215)

About the Qualities of a Ruler:
O God, You certainly know that the ruler who is in charge of honor, lives, wealth, law, and order should not be a miser or a greedy individual, for then he would misappropriate wealth; nor should he be ignorant, for then he would mislead his subjects; nor should he be of rude nature, for he would then estrange his subjects; nor should he be inequitable, preferring one group over another. He should not accept bribes while making decisions, for he would then forfeit rights (of others), nor should he ignore the Prophet's teaching, as he would ruin the faith.
(Sermon 130)

Letter to a High Official:
Give up extravagance and be moderate in expenditure (with public funds). Do not let the pleasures of today make you forget tomorrow, the Day of Reckoning (Judgment). Distribute excess monies (beyond the needs of the government) to the poor, so that it may act as a provision for you in the next world. Do you expect God to grant you rewards reserved for courteous, kind, and benevolent people while you actually are proud, vain, haughty, and miserly? Do you hope to receive His Blessings reserved for charitable, generous, and kindhearted persons who always help the poor and the needy, while you indulge in luxuries and prevent any part of your wealth from reaching the disabled, the widows, and the destitute?

Remember, a person receives the reward in the next world according to the actions in this world.
(Letter 21)

Letter to the Judge of a Province:

> Imam Ali (p) learned that the Chief Justice of a province had purchased a very expensive house for an amount far below market price from an individual (probably) seeking a favor in return. Imam Ali (p) summoned him and warned him that this deal was made with money that was not his. He warned him that this would make him lose a place in Paradise. Had the Chief Justice consulted him, the Imam would have disapproved the deal.

If you had come to me prior to this transaction, I would have drafted such a deed of sale for you that you would not have cared to purchase this property even for a small fraction of the cost. The transfer deed would have been worded like this:

"A humble and powerless creature has purchased this house from another mortal being. Its boundaries are as follows: On one side, it is bounded by calamities and disasters; on the other side, there is disappointment and grief; on the third side it is bounded by excessive desires leading to failure; and on the fourth side, it has the allurements of Satan. The door of this house opens towards this fourth side.

"A man leading his life under the merciless grip of desire has purchased this house from another person who is being relentlessly pursued by death. For the purchase price, he has exchanged the glory of an honorably contented and respectable way of living, with the detestable life of submitting to every form of humiliation for profits and pleasures.

"His fate now lies in the hands of Him (Almighty God) Who sends the bodies of kings into dust and overthrows their empires, and Who has brought to an end the dominions of ancient Egypt, Persia, Greece, Rome, and the kings of Yemen. He destroyed the wealth, power, and glory of all those individuals who had amassed excessive wealth, built mansions, furnished them luxuriously, and surrounded them with beautiful gardens. The owner of such properties will have to account for on the Day of Judgment, the day on which evildoers will suffer for their wicked ways." **(Letter 3)**

Instructions to a Newly Appointed Young Governor of Egypt:

Treat people with respect and be kind and considerate. Meet them cheerfully. Be fair, just, and impartial in your dealings, so that the influential persons may not dare take undue advantage of your leniency, and the ordinary folks and the poor may not feel ignored.

O creature of God! Remember that the Almighty Lord is going to take an account of each of your sins, be they major or minor, committed openly or secretly. If He punishes you, it will be His justice, and if He forgives you, it will be because of His Great Mercy and Forgiveness.

Remember, the pious passed away from this world after having led a respectable and fruitful life, and they are going to be rewarded in the next world. While leaving the world, they carried provisions that would be of use in the next world.

Fear death; it is inevitable and near. Be prepared to meet it. Verily, it will come as the most important and the greatest event of your life; it will bring blessings and rewards (of the Hereafter) for you, or it will bring in its wake punishment, suffering, and eternal damnation. There will be no chance of redemption (after death). It is for you to decide whether to proceed towards perpetual peace and blessings, or towards damnation. Remember that life is actually driving you towards death. Death is as if it is wound around your neck, and life is as if it is being unwound with each breath.

Hell is an abode where the prayers and pleadings of those thrown there will not be accepted (because they died unrepentant).

Fear (disconnecting from) God, as well as have hope in His Justice, Mercy, and Love. Hold these two beliefs (i.e., hope and fear) equally. An individual entertains and cherishes the love, reverence, and veneration of God in proportion to His fear and awe that develops in his mind.

Remember, I have entrusted you with the command of the most important section of my army, which is the Egyptian army. Do not allow your whims and passions to overcome your judgment. Keep on guarding and defending your religion and the State given under your trust. Be careful, for in order to gain the pleasure of a person, you should not incur the Wrath of God upon you for even a single moment.

Remember that the Pleasure of God is better than the pleasure of all His subjects (combined), and most beneficial for you. Nothing can take the place of His good pleasure. Offer your (obligatory) prayers on time, do not rush through them, and never delay in offering them. Remember that the God-consciousness and nobility of your actions are judged by the sincerity and punctuality of your (obligatory) prayers.

Remember that a true Imam and leader cannot be equated with the one who leads humanity towards wickedness, vice, and Hellfire.

Nor can they be equal: A follower of the Prophet (s), and his sworn enemy.

(Letter 27)

Letter to the Governor of Basra in Iraq:

I have received information that a person of Basra invited you to a dinner and you immediately accepted the invitation. I have also heard that very sumptuous meals were served there. The finest varieties of viands were placed before you in large plates, and you enjoyed them. I am sorry to hear the news. I never expected that you would accept the invitation of a person who invites big officers and rich people, but from whose doors the poor, the destitute, and the hungry are rudely turned away.

Look carefully into the things that you eat. If there is even a trace of their being obtained unlawfully, then throw them away. Eat only those things about which you are certain that they are obtained by honest means. Every follower of religion has a leader from whom to learn the canons of the religion and the ways of leading a pious life.

Happy is the person who performed his duty to God and to people, who bore adversities patiently, and, when sleep overpowered him, he used his hand as a pillow and lay on mere earth along with those whom fear of the Day of Judgment has often kept awake. He does not find much time to sleep; his lips are busy glorifying God, and his sins have been absolved because of repentance. He is a noble person and he will secure salvation. Therefore, be God-conscious and be content with the bread that you get with lawful means, so that you may be saved from punishment on the Day of Judgment.

(Letter 45)

Letter to a Companion:

This world is like a serpent; it is soft (pleasant) to touch, yet lethal in its bite. Therefore, try to avoid those things of this world that please and allure you, because this world will be with you for a very short period (only). Do not let your mind be fully occupied in mundane affairs, because you know that you will soon leave this world.

Be most wary and cautious of this world, because when it pleases you the most and you are happy with it and feel secure, it will suddenly forsake you.
(Letter 68)

Letter to a High Government Official:
Never forsake the ordinances and advice contained in the Qur'an. Accept the rulings therein regarding the lawful and the prohibited. Take lessons from history, for history often repeats itself.

This whole world is eventually going to end and every individual has to leave it (at the appointed time). Be particularly careful not to swear by God Almighty, unless you are taking an oath for a true and lawful affair. Always remember death (be prepared for it), but never wish for it.

Abstain from an act done secretly that will make you feel ashamed if done openly. Refrain from a deed for which you will have regret and have to make an apology or an excuse. Do not allow your good reputation to be sullied. Do not accept rumors (unverified) as facts, for such a practice will be sufficient for you to be regarded by others as a liar. Do not develop the habit of contradicting and falsifying others on every occasion, because it is a disgusting habit.

Control your temper, and even if you have power to retaliate, (it is better to) forgive and forget.[1] When in anger, try to be forbearing and tolerant. Despite being in possession of wealth and authority, be forgiving, merciful, and compassionate. These qualities will help you to achieve salvation. Be sincerely thankful for all the blessings that the

---

1 *"We have prescribed for them (in retaliation) therein, a life for a life, an eye for an eye… but whoever remits it (foregoes by way of charity), it shall be an expiation (atonement) for his/her sins"* (Qur'an 5:45).

Merciful God has granted you. Pray for the continuance of the blessings; do not abuse and squander them.

Always look at the conditions of people who are less well off than you, because observing their lives will make you more content with your lot in life and make you more thankful to God (for your blessings).

Do not travel on Fridays without offering Friday prayers, unless there is a state of war or you have no other alternative.

Take care that such a calamity may not overtake you that while you are ignoring religious obligations and (heedless of duties to) God, and running after vanities of the world, death (suddenly) overtakes you.

Be afraid of your anger, because out of all the weapons of Satan, inciting anger (in a person) is his strongest (weapon).
(Letter 69)

Letter to a Corrupt Official:
I have received reliable information that you do not check and control your excessive desires, that you do not attach any importance to your life after death, that you want to adorn and beautify your life at the cost of your salvation, and that you are forsaking your religion in order to benefit your relatives. Men of your disposition are not to be trusted with financial affairs, or to be appointed to important posts of the State. Therefore, as soon as you receive this letter, come back to see me.
(Letter 71)

Instructions to the Governor of a Province with Disloyal People:
Treat people kindly, receive them in audience, and do not be harsh in issuing and enforcing orders. Do not lose your temper, because this allows Satan to find his way into your mind. Always keep this in mind: that the thing that takes you near to God will move you away

from Hell, and the thing that drives you away from God will drive you towards Hell.
(Letter 76)

Instruction to an Official Dealing with Dissenters:

While arguing, never quote statements from the Qur'an, because the passages of this Book require careful study and deliberation, as they could be paraphrased in various ways and their meanings could be construed differently. Therefore, argue with them in the light of the traditions of the Prophet (s), and then they will find no way to misrepresent the truth.
(Letter 77)

HIS INSTRUCTIONS TO ARMY OFFICERS

Introduction: The Prophet Muhammad (s) had to fight many defensive battles during his ministry. He prohibited wars of aggression or initiating hostilities. Imam Ali (p), as the head of state, strictly enforced the teachings of the Prophet (s). Furthermore, his orders to the commanders and soldiers show the highest degree of humane treatment and respect to the captured enemy, the wounded, women, and children. Such exemplary standards of conducting war are vastly different from what we observe around the world in modern wars that lead to mayhem, ruthlessness, and killing of civilians.

Instruction to Soldiers before a Battle:
You do not initiate the fighting, but let the enemy begin it, because, by the Grace of God, you are on the side of truth and justice. Let them begin their hostilities and then you are at liberty to fight. Their willingness to start the fighting will be another proof of your sincere belief in obeying God.

If God favors you with success and inflicts defeat on the enemy, then do not attack those who have surrendered, do not injure the disabled and weak, do not assault the wounded, do not treat women rudely even if they use harsh and insulting words against your commander and officers, because they get excited easily and frightened quickly. During the days of the Prophet (s), we had strict orders not to touch, molest, or insult women even though they were unbelievers.
(Letter 14)

A Circular to the Chiefs of His Army:

This letter is from the servant of God, Ali bin Abu Talib, to the chiefs of his army and generals of his cantonments.

My duty towards you is that, except for the classified information regarding war-related matters, I should not keep any information about the affairs of the State hidden from you. Except questions related to religious matters, I should take you in my confidence and seek your advice in all other affairs. I should safeguard your interests and rights to the best of my ability, I should see that you are well protected and well looked after, and I should treat all of you equally without any favoritism. Your obedience to me is that you follow my orders, (strive to) be good, and courageously face difficulties to attain the right path. If you cannot maintain this standard of fidelity, then you will lose the straight path, the path of virtue, and you will lose position in my eyes. I will order punishment for you in that case. You should make sure that your subordinate officers act accordingly, and you should give them the similar facilities and privileges as are given to you, so that your affairs also run smoothly.
(Letter 50)

Instructions to the Commander of a Force Heading to the Battlefront:

(I advise you to) be God-conscious at all times, be it day or night. Be cautious of the alluring and cruel world and never trust it. Check your desire of acquiring excessive things of the world (booty); otherwise, your desires will surely lead you towards loss. (I advise you) to control anger and do not lose your temper.
(Letter 56)

HIS FISCAL POLICIES, INSTRUCTIONS TO TAX COLLECTORS

Introduction: Imam Ali (p) laid down strict rules for handling public funds. The highest degree of honesty and integrity was expected from his officials and tax collectors. Tax collectors were required to show civility, generosity, and fairness in dealing with the taxpayers.

Warning against Misappropriation of Public Funds, Even When Faced with Poverty:
By God, I would rather pass a night in wakefulness on thorns, or be driven in chains as a prisoner, than meet God and His Messenger on the Day of Judgment as an oppressor over any person or a usurper of any worldly wealth. How can I oppress anyone for (the sake of) the life that is proceeding towards the end (death), and will be buried under the earth and remain there for a long period?
(Sermon 222)

More about Public Funds:
This money (in the public treasury) is not for me or for you, but it is the collective property of the people.
(Sermon 230)

Admonition to the Commissioner of a Province:
I swear by God that if I find you misappropriating the wealth (from the public treasury), I will punish you in such a way that you will end up poor. Besides, there will be the burden of sin on your shoulders, you will be disgraced and humiliated, and you will lose your position and prestige.
(Letter 20)

Excerpts from a Letter to Tax Collectors:

I instruct you to be God-conscious in all affairs and on all occasions, even where there is none to witness your actions and deeds, or to guide your activities. Do not feign God-consciousness and then disobey God's ordinances. One whose deeds agree with his words and who is as honest in secret as in public, he is the person who has faithfully discharged his duty laid down upon him by the Lord. He has honestly handled the things entrusted to him, and he is sincere in seeking God's favors and blessings.

I instruct you not to oppress the people (the taxpayers), do not deal with them harshly, and do not ill-treat them. As a result, they will (fully) cooperate with you and will help you in your task.
(Letter 26)

His Directive to Tax Collectors:

Do not give up being God-conscious, and (know that) He has no partner. Do not bring grief to people (by your actions), and do not make them dislike you. Do not overtax them.

When you reach a group of people (tribe or village) to assess taxes, do not stay in their houses. Go to them maintaining your dignity and prestige, and when you are in their midst, wish them peace and blessings of God and show them due respect. Inform them that the Caliph has sent you to collect from them their dues (religious tax). Ask them whether they possess enough means to pay the dues. If someone tells you that he does not possess enough wealth to make him liable to pay taxes, then do not bother him, and accept his plea. If someone tells you he is in a position to pay the tax, collect the tax in cash or kind (as the case may be). Do not frighten or make him nervous, and do not deal with him harshly.

While assessing tax on cattle and other livestock, do not tyrannize the owner or frighten the animals. Once the animals have been secured, assign them to an honest person to deliver them to the state authority. Entrust them to a person who is trustworthy and who is of a kind nature, so that he may not mistreat the animals or starve or tire out the animals during the transit.

Instruct him not to separate a she-camel from its young, not to milk it so much that nothing is left for its young one, and not to drive them harshly or overburden them with excessive load. He should always give them enough rest at watering places. They should not be driven through deserts as much as possible, and should follow green lands and regions with plenty of wooded areas. Thus, every care should be taken so that they reach their destination in healthy and robust condition. Verily, the collection of the dues (ordained by God) in the way that I have explained to you is a deed of God-consciousness and a religious duty that will carry its reward before the Lord.
(Letter 25)

8. TO PREPARE FOR THE PERMANENT ABODE (AFTERLIFE)

Life of This World, the Hereafter, and Death

About Paradise

LIFE OF THIS WORLD, THE HEREAFTER, AND DEATH

Introduction: The Islamic concept of life (of this world) refers to a temporary state of being, a period of test and trial. It is not meant for indulging in luxuries and excesses. Rather, it is for preparing for an eternal life in the Hereafter. Death is the beginning of the next phase of life, the everlasting life, "the real life." There are detailed accounts of the life in the Hereafter recorded in the Qur'an and in the sermons of Prophet Muhammad (s). In the following pages, Imam Ali (p) eloquently expounds upon these concepts as a warning and guidance to humanity. His deep knowledge and understanding of the Qur'an and the teachings of the Prophet are evident here. His understanding of God's workings is an indicator of his high level of spiritual insight.

Transient Nature of This World:

Surely this world will depart, and the next world will take its place. "Today" is the day of preparation, while "tomorrow" will be the day of the race (to the destination). Paradise is the place of bliss, whereas Hell is the place of doom. Is there anyone to repent for his sins before his death? Is there anyone to perform virtuous acts (atonement) before the Day of trial?

You entertain many hopes, but beware; death is not far behind you. Whoever acts righteously will reap the benefits, and the approaching death will not bring harm to him/her. However, whoever fails to act righteously before the approach of death, he will be in a loss, and his/her death will bring harm. Beware; act (prudently) during a period of ease, just as you would act during a period of difficulty. Beware; surely

I have not seen one who desires Paradise, or one who dreads Hell to be in sleep (of heedlessness). Beware; he whom right (goodness) does not benefit must suffer the harm of the wrong (evil), and he whom guidance does not keep steady (on the right path) will be the victim of misguidance and destruction.

Beware; you have been destined to journey relentlessly (to meet your Lord), and you have been advised to collect provision for that. Surely the most frightening thing is to pursue (vain) desires and to have inflated hopes. Gather Provision from the world that you will need tomorrow (on the Day of Judgment).
(Sermon 28)

Beware! An action that is performed only for earning benefit in this world will not earn benefit in the Hereafter. People are tested in this world through (loss and) calamities. The worldly pleasures here will be terminated (by death), and people will be asked about the pleasures. Whatever (good deeds) they have performed, they will find them in the next world.
(Sermon 62)

O creatures of God! In this world, you are like guests with a limited duration of stay. Many people are wasting (their time and efforts) and are putting themselves in harm's way. You belong to a period where virtue is on the wane, evil is on the rise, and Satan is doubling his effort to ruin the people.

Cast your glance over people wherever you like; you will see either a poor individual suffering from poverty, or a rich person heedless of God (His presence) while enjoying His bounties. You will see a miser increasing his wealth by trampling on his obligations to God, or an unruly person closing his ears to good counsel. Where are your good people?

Admonishing a Certain Group of People:
"Where are your virtuous people? Where are your high-spirited and generous men? Where are those of you who avoid deceit in their

business and remain pure in their behavior? Have they not all departed from this ignoble, transitory, and troublesome world? God says this in the Scripture: *"Verily we are God's (belong to God) and verily unto Him shall we return"* **(Qur'an 2:156)**
(Sermon 12)

I advise you, O creatures of God, that you be God-conscious, and I warn you about this world, which is a house from which departure is inevitable.

O creatures of God, you should know now that you have to perform (good) acts, because (at present) your have freedom of speech, and your bodies are healthy (and strong). Consider this: death is inevitable.
(Sermon 195)

Lowliness of this World:
The destruction of this world is preordained, and its inhabitants are destined to depart from it. It is sweet and attractive. It hastens towards its seeker and tends to be attractive to their hearts. So, do not seek here more than what is reasonable; depart from this world with the best provision (for the Hereafter).
(Sermon 45)

About the Fall and Destruction of this World:
O creatures of God, be prepared to leave this world, for your abode is your grave. Beware lest your heart's desires overpower you. Do not consider your stay in this world to be an extended one. Turn to God, seek His nearness, and strive for an honorable position with Him. Pray for the forgiveness of your sins, as recorded by the Angels.

O creatures of God, purchase the everlasting joy (of the Hereafter) by foregoing transitory pleasures of this world. You are being driven towards death, which is hovering over you. Certainly God has not created you without purpose. Every moment that is passing by is shortening your life. Gather provision from this world today which you will need tomorrow (in the afterlife).

Therefore, we ask God, the Glorified, that He does not allow us to be seduced by bounties of this world, that nothing will prevent us from His obedience (and submission), and that shame and grief do not befall us after death.
(Sermon 63)

About the World and Worldly People:
In what way shall I describe the (life of the) world? Its beginning is grief and its end is destruction. The lawful actions performed here have to be accounted for, while for the forbidden actions, there is punishment (in the Hereafter, if not forgiven). Whoever is rich here encounters mischief and whoever is poor suffers from grief. He who hankers after it (the World) does not get it, and the one who stays away from it, it advances towards him. If one sees through it, it would bestow him insight, but if one has his eye set on it, then it blinds him.
(Sermon 81)

I warn you of this world, for it has decorated itself with deceptions. God regards it lowly. In it, lawful with unlawful are mixed, good with evil, life with death, and its sweetness with its bitterness. Its habitations would ultimately face desolation. What good is a house that is destined for destruction?

Ask God for the fulfillment of what He has made obligatory on you. The remembrance of death has disappeared from your hearts, while false hopes have beguiled you. Therefore, this world has mastered you more than the next world. Although you are brethren in the religion of God, you do not share the burdens of each other, nor do you advise each other, nor do you spend your wealth to help, nor do you love each other.

What is your condition? You feel satisfied with what you have secured from this world, while you are oblivious of your loss in the next world. If you lose a little from this world, it grieves you much and you show lack of patience over what is taken away, as though this is your

permanent abode. You have fallen in love with this world and have become heedless of the next world.
(Sermon 112)

Various Types of People in the World and about the World's Lowliness:
O people! We live in such a time, wherein the virtuous are regarded as base and the oppressor is allowed to commit excesses. We do not make use of what we know and do not discover what we do not know. We do not fear calamity until it befalls us.

There is a person who is prevented from making mischief because of his low position in society and lack of resources. He calls it contentment and renunciation, although he has never had any connection with these (noble) qualities.

Then there is the one who has drawn his sword, openly commits mischief, and has devoted himself to securing wealth, power, and position. He has allowed his faith to perish. How bad is the transaction that you choose (the enjoyment of) this world in exchange for what God has for you (in the Hereafter)!

There are some people to whom the thought of their return (to God) makes them humble and the fear of the Day of resurrection moves them to tears. Some of them are frightened and subdued, some are quiet and restrained in their speech, and some are praying sincerely. They (strive to) preach (goodness), but they are harassed (by those in power). Some are unjustly killed, and a few (manage to) survive.

The (value of the) world in your eyes should be "less than the bark of the acacia plant"[1] (i.e., worthless). Take a lesson from those who went ahead of you (departed from this world).
(Sermon 32)

---

1 Meaning the material possessions of the world have no value in the Eternal life in the Hereafter. They might even be a liability unless spent in charity and human welfare.

Reason for Our Creation:

O creatures of God, be God-conscious; be aware of the reason that He has created you. Make yourself deserving of (bounties) that God has promised you by putting Trust in God, and by fearing the Day of Judgment. **(Sermon 82)**

In answer to a question, Imam Ali said this: "The Universe without plan, purpose, and program is the idea of infidels and the pagans; sorry will be their plight in the leaping fires of Hell." Hearing this, the man asked Imam Ali, "Then what kind of destiny was it that we had?" Imam Ali replied: "It was an order of God to do it like the order He has given in His Holy Book: You are destined by God to worship none but Him,[1] and here 'destined' means 'ordered.' It does not mean physical compulsion" **(A Saying)**

Advice on Abstinence (from Indulging in Luxuries) and about the Changing Times:

We praise God for what has already passed and seek His succor in our affairs for what is yet to come, and we beseech Him to safeguard our faith, just as we beseech Him to safeguard our bodies.

O creatures of God! I advise you to keep away from (luxuries of) this world, which you will (shortly) have to leave, even though you may not be ready for it.

Do not hanker after worldly honor and pride, and do not feel elated over its adornments and bounties, nor wail over its losses and misfortunes, because its honor and pride will end, while its beauty and bounty will perish. Everything in it will come to an end, and every living being in it is (destined) to die. Is there not for you a warning in the relics of your predecessors? Do you not see that your predecessors do not come back?

---

1 "You (God) alone do we worship, and from You (only) do we seek help" (Qur'an 1:5).

Beware! At the time of committing evil deeds, remember the destroyer of joys, the spoiler of pleasures, and the killer of desires (i.e., death). Seek assistance from God for the fulfillment of His obligatory rights and for (thanking Him) for His countless bounties and favors.
(Sermon 98)

O people! Look at those who abstain and turn away from the worldly desires. By God, it would shortly cause grief to the happy and the (ones who consider themselves) safe. The one who goes away from it never returns. That which is to happen, (the time of death) is not known, nor can it be anticipated. The joys (of this world) are mixed with grief.

May God shower His Mercy on him who ponders (over the affairs), takes lesson from it, and thereby achieves enlightenment. Whatever exists in this world will (eventually) become nonexistent, while whatever is to be in the next world already exists.
(Sermon 102)

Cautioning Against the World's Deceptions:

I caution you about this world, for it is sweet and attractive, surrounded by lusts and sought for its immediate enjoyments. It excites wonder, is ornamented with (false) hopes, and is decorated with deceptions. Its rejoicing does not last for long, and its afflictions cannot be avoided. It is deceitful, changing, perishable, exhaustible, and destructive. About the one who achieves the (worldly) desires and feels happy with it, God, the Glorified, says (in the Qur'an):

"Like the water which We send down from heaven, and the herbage of the earth mingleth with it, then it becometh dry stubble which the winds scatter; for God, over all things, hath power." **(Qur'an Chapter 18:45)**

No person derives pleasure from this world without experiencing sadness afterwards, and no one enjoys its comforts without encountering hardships later on. In the morning, it supports an individual, but in the evening, it does not recognize him. If one side of it is sweet and pleasant, then the other side is bitter and distressing.

No one secures enjoyment from its freshness, but (subsequently) has to face hardship from its calamities. No one would pass the evening in safety, but that the morning would bring fear. It is filled with deception, and everything on it will perish. The best provision therein is God-consciousness. How many people relied on this world, but it caused them distress; and (how many) felt peaceful in it, but it let them down; how many achieved prestige in it, but it brought them low, and how many felt proud of it, but they fell in disgrace?

Its authority is ever changing and its sweetness turns bitter. The healthy in it are liable to disease, the strong in it are (liable to be) defeated, and the rich are (liable to be) afflicted with misfortune. Are you not (residing) in the houses of those who went before you? How they devoted themselves to the world and were attracted by it! Then they left (empty-handed) without any provision for the next world.

You should know that (eventually) you have to depart from this world. Therefore, while in it, take lessons from those who had proclaimed:

"Who is more powerful than we (the boastful)?" **(Qur'an 41:15).**

However, they were carried to their abodes in their graves.
(Sermon 119)

Beware of the Trap:
Certainly, this world's appearance is attractive and its inside is destructive. It is full of deceptions and mirages. When one begins to like it and feels comfortable, it puts down its foot and catches (its victim) in its trap.
(Sermon 82)

About How This World Treats Those Who are Attached to It:

Know that this world which you have started to covet, in which you are interested, which sometimes enrages you and sometimes pleases you, it is not your (permanent) abode. Turn your hearts away from this world and do not grieve over what you have been deprived in it.

Know that the loss of anything of this world will not harm you if you have safeguarded the principles of your religion. Know also that after the loss of your religion, nothing of this world will benefit you. May God guide our hearts to what is right, and may He grant us endurance.

(Sermon 172)

About Collecting Provision for the Next World:

O people, certainly this world is (like) a passage, whereas the next world is a place of permanent abode. So, from the passage, take (all you can for the permanent abode), because you have been created for the next world. When a man dies, people ask, "What (property) has he?" while the angels ask, "What (good actions) has he sent forward?" May God bless you, send in advance something (for the next world); it will be credited to you, and the (material possessions) you leave behind will be a liability for you (on the Day of Judgment).

(Sermon 202)

Death and Resurrection

The people are marching towards their death. God would then bring them out (on the resurrection day) from their graves. They will respond to His command and hasten towards the assigned places, in groups. They will be speechless, standing in rows, and within God's sight.

They will be in a state of helplessness, submission, and humility. Their cleverness will disappear, their hearts will sink, their throats will choke, they will be overcome with fear, and their ears will resound with the

thundering voice of the announcer, calling them towards the (seat of) judgment to receive recompense for good deeds, or to receive punishment.
(Sermon 82)

Spiritual Aspects of Death and Preparation for the Day of Judgment:

Are the people who are in youth now waiting for (inevitable) old age to arrive? Are those currently enjoying good health waiting for (unexpected) ailments to afflict? Are those who are alive anticipating the encounter with death? When the hour of death would be close, it will be the time to look to relatives and friends for help (and support). Could then the near ones stop (or reverse) death, or would the mourning be of any good? All the dead will end up in the grave. Then, neither can good acts be added to nor can sins be atoned by repentance. Are you not sons, fathers, brothers, and relations of the dead? Are you not to follow them in the same manner? However, hearts are still not moved (to take lessons), being heedless of guidance and moving in the wrong direction, as though the right thing to do is to amass worldly gains.

Know that (on the Day of Judgment) you have to pass over the pathway (Bridge of siraat)[1] where steps waver, feet slip away, and there are fears and dangers at every step. O creatures of God, be God-conscious, like the fearing of a wise man whom the thought (of the next world) has turned away from other (lesser) matters, fear (of reckoning) has afflicted his body with anxiety and pain, abstention has curbed his worldly desires, and remembrance of God is ever on his tongue. He avoids crooked ways in favor of clear ones. He follows the shortest route to secure his purpose, wishfulness does not distort his thinking, and ambiguities do not blind his eyes. He enjoys restful sleep and passes his day content because of the (anticipation of) the good tidings and the pleasures (in the

1 A narrow bridge on which humankind will be made to journey on the Day of Judgment. The sinners will falter, whereas the righteous will have an easy passage.

Hereafter). He passes the pathway of this world in a praiseworthy manner. He reaches the next world with virtues. He hastens (towards virtue) out of fear (of falling in vices). He devotes himself in seeking (eternal) benefit and shuns evil. He keeps the future in his view. Certainly Paradise is a reward and an achievement, while Hell is (a place of) punishment and suffering. God is the Reckoner, and the Helper, and the Qur'an is the best argument and a confronter (of those who disobey).
(Sermon 82)

The Lesson to Learn from Those Who Have Passed Away:
O creatures of God! Where are those who were allowed (long) ages and enjoyed the bounties? They were given time and they wasted it in vain (pursuits); they were bestowed with health, but they forgot (their duty). They were allowed a long period (of life), they were warned of punishment and were promised great rewards. Therefore, you should avoid sins that lead to destruction and vices that prompt the wrath (of God).

O people, O possessors of eyes, ears, health, and wealth; is there any place of refuge, any shelter in which to find safety, any safe haven, or any opportunity to escape (death), or to return back (to this world)? God asks the deniers in the Qur'an this:

"He brings out the living from the dead, and the dead from the living. That is God! How are you then turned away deluded?" **(Qur'an 6:95).**

(O people) what has deceived you? Certainly, your share from this earth is just a piece of land, the size of your grave; you will lie there covered with dust. The present (time) is an opportune moment to act (righteously).

O creatures of God, since you are enjoying leisure and freedom, now is the time to seek guidance. You are free to assemble and have freedom of action, so use the opportunity to seek forgiveness before you are overtaken by hard times, distresses, fear, infirmity, or death.

O creatures of God! Derive benefit from the preaching and admonitions. Your march is towards the place where everyone has to go, namely, your grave. The Qur'an says:

"With every person there is a driver and a witness"[1] **(Qur'an 50:21).**

The driver drives him towards the day of resurrection, while the witness furnishes evidence about his deeds. **(Sermon 82)**

They were ignoring it (death), but it struck, causing their separation from this world. They reached their destination (in the next world) as they were promised, and their fate is unknown to their kinsfolk.

Death stands between him/her and the people; He (the soul) is able to see and able to hear. He (the soul) then ponders over how he wasted his life and in what (activities) he passed his time. He recalls the wealth he collected, (if he) was blinded with greed in seeking it, and whether he acquired it by fair or unfair means. Now the consequences of amassing wealth have overtaken him. He has to leave his wealth behind for the next of kin. They would enjoy his wealth (oblivious of his suffering).

(What he bequeaths) would be a bonanza for the recipients, but it will be a burden (of accountability) on his back, and he will not be able to escape the accountability. He will thereupon bite his fingertips out of shame (and remorse) when his deeds will be shown to him. He will regret what he coveted during his life and will wish that someone other than him/her had owned that wealth.
(Sermon 108)

We praise God for whatever He takes away from us (or denies) and whatever He grants us; whatever He inflicts upon us, or with whatever He tries us. He is (fully) aware of all that is hidden, and He sees all that is concealed. He knows all that the hearts and the eyes hide.

---

1 The angels will be the drivers and Witnesses over each person on the Day of Judgment.

We testify that there is no god except He, that Muhammad (s) is His chosen (messenger), and he was sent by Him (as guidance to humanity).

By God, certainly, death is a reality. You have seen those who lived before you; they amassed wealth, and then death overtook them; it took them out of the safety of their homes.

Did you not witness those who were busy in achieving their desires? They built big and strong buildings, amassed much wealth, but their death led them to their graves, and their collections turned into ruin. Their Estate was inherited by those left behind. Therefore, whoever makes his/her heart to be God-conscious achieves a forward position, and his/her efforts are successful. Thus, prepare yourself for the Hereafter and do all that you can to achieve Paradise. Certainly this world has not been designated as a place of permanent stay for you. It is made as a passage in order that you may take from it the provisions (your good deeds) for your permanent abode (in the Hereafter). Prepare yourself for departure from this world.
(Sermon 131)

Learn from Those Who Have Already Passed Away:
I also advise you to remember death and to lessen your heedlessness towards it. Those who died before you should suffice as examples. They were carried to their graves by others. They vacated the places where they lived, and they now lie in a lonely place (the grave). Now, they cannot escape from the consequences of their sinful deeds, nor can they add to their good deeds. They attached themselves to the world, but it deceived them. They trusted it, but it abandoned them.
(Sermon 187)

About the Angel of Death:
Do you see him, when the Angel of death enters a house, and when he draws the life out of an individual? Do you know how he takes the life out of an embryo in the womb of its mother? Does he reach the

embryo in the mother's interior? Thus, how would he, who is unable to describe (or understand) a creature like this, be able to describe God?
(Sermon 111)

About the Dead and Their Condition in the Graves:
Those who have died have reached their goal and have arrived at their destination ahead of you. They had held positions of honor and pride (in this world). Some of them were rulers and others held high positions. Now they lie lifeless in their graves. The approach of (earthly) dangers does not frighten them anymore, earthquakes do not bother them, nor do they pay heed to thunderstorms.

Their situation is unknown to those who are left behind; they were made to drink the cup (of death), which has changed their speech into silence, their hearing turned into deafness, and their movements into stillness. It seems as though they are fallen in slumber. Every one of them is in a lonely place (the grave), unaware of the time of the day or night. Their faces and bodies are covered with dust. Those who are still alive should draw lessons from them.
(Sermon 219)

ABOUT PARADISE

Introduction: The concept of the afterlife and the reward of Paradise is part of the belief system of many religions. The Qur'an gives many details about the heavenly bounties. It also describes the blessed ones who will enter Paradise. Imam Ali (p), in these few paragraphs, gives a summary of the pleasures of Paradise and the way to achieve them. Some details are amazing and cause one to wonder if he actually visited Paradise, or perhaps learned it from the Prophet (s), who ascended to the highest levels of Heaven on the night of *Me'raj* (ascension).[1]

Paradise, an Everlasting Abode:
In Paradise, there are different places (levels) of residence. Its boundaries have no limits. He or she who stays in it will never have to move out of it. He who is blessed will never be in need of anything else.
(Sermon 84)

A Description of Paradise:
If you cast your mind's eye at what is described to you about Paradise, your heart would begin to dislike the pleasures and adornments of this world. You would be lost in the rustling of the trees of Paradise, whose roots lie hidden in the mounds of musk on the banks of the rivers, and in the sight of different fruits from under the cover of their leaves. These fruits can be picked without difficulty, as they come down at the desire of the inhabitants. Pure honey will be handed around to those who settle down in the courtyards of its palaces.

---

1 Please refer to the glossary section.

They are honorable people who are made to settle in the house of eternal abode, and they have rested there from their journey. O you listeners, if you busy yourself in advancing towards those wonderful scenes which will rush towards you, then your heart's desire will be to die in eagerness for them. O God, by Your Mercy, include us also among those who strive with their hearts for the abodes of the virtuous.
(Sermon 164)

An Invitation to Paradise:
Glorified are You, O the Creator, the one worshipped. You created a house (Paradise) and provided (facilities) in it for feasting, refreshing drinks, mates, servants, streams, plantations, and fruits. Then You sent a messenger to invite people towards it, but many people did not respond to the caller and did not show eagerness towards what You offered them. They jumped on the wagon (of the transient pleasures), they loved this world, and they earned shame (in the Hereafter).
(Sermon 108)

9. ALI'S DISCOURSES ON OTHER TOPICS

About Prophet Muhammad (s)

About Other Prophets

Imam Ali (p) about Himself

About the Family of Muhammad (s)

About Islam

About the Scripture, the Qur'an

K'aba (The House of God) and the Hajj Pilgrimage

Islamic Ritual Prayers (Salaat)

About Satan

About Divisiveness

About Faith, Disbelief, and Doubt

Miscellaneous Topics

ABOUT PROPHET MUHAMMAD (S)

Introduction: Much has been written about Prophet Muhammad (s), the last Prophet of God. Imam Ali (p) is uniquely positioned to expound on the personality of the prophet due to his close relationship to him. He was not only the cousin but also the son-in-law of the Prophet (s). Imam Ali (p) was also raised by the Prophet and was his companion and confidant. As such, Imam Ali (p) assumed the role of the Prophet's protector and faithful bodyguard. In addition to being constantly in the Prophet's presence, Ali (p) was privy to the divine knowledge revealed to the Prophet (s).

God Chooses His Prophets:
From his (Adam's) progeny, God chose prophets and took their pledge for his revelation and for carrying His message as a trust. However, people perverted the trust (message) after having received it. Satan turned people away from the truth of God and distracted them from His worship. God sent His Messengers (Prophets who also brought divine books) and a series of prophets to humankind to fulfill the pledge (worship only God Almighty), to remind them about His bounties, to exhort them to God's way, to teach them virtues, and to show them the signs of His Omnipotence. Examples of His signs of Omnipotence are the sky that is raised over them, the earth that is placed beneath them, their means of livelihood, the ailments, old age and infirmity, their mishaps that betake them, and, finally, death (that ends the worldly existence).

God never allowed His creation to remain without a Prophet sent by Him, or a book (message) sent down by Him. These Messengers were

such that they did not deter (in proclaiming the message) despite strong forces that opposed them. The prophets and messengers designated their successors according to divine command.
(Sermon 1)

About the Prophethood of Muhammad (s):
Finally, God sent Muhammad (s) as His Prophet, in fulfillment of His promise and concluding the line of prophethood. His character was matchless and his ancestry was honorable. The people of the earth at his time were divided into different groups; their aims and their ways were diverse. They joined other gods with God (polytheism). Through Muhammad, God guided them out of sin and ignorance.
(Sermon 1)

His Invocation of Blessings on Prophet Muhammad (s):
O my God, O the Creator and Sustainer of the heavens and the earth, send ever-increasing blessings and favors on Muhammad, Your servant and Your prophet, the last and the final prophet of God. He proclaimed truth and repulsed the forces of wrong, and defeated the forces of misguidance. He bore the burden (of prophethood), submitting to Your commands, and fulfilled Your Will with steadfastness and determination. He received and acknowledged your revelations, preserved Your testament, took the lead in spreading Your commands, and lighted the path for the seekers of truth that were groping in the darkness (of ignorance).

He is Your envoy, bearing the truth, and Your Messenger to humankind. O my God, grant him an exalted place in the shade (of Your Mercy), and award him ever-increasing blessings and bounties.

O my God, for his carrying out your mandate faithfully, grant perfection to his light. My God, bestow on us Your blessings, increase bounties, satisfy our needs and desires, remove difficulties, grant us ease of living, peace of mind, and the gift of an honorable stay (in this life).
(Sermon 71)

About His Mission:
God sent the Prophet (s) when the mission of other prophets had concluded earlier and people were in slumber (of heedlessness) for a long time. Evil was raising its head, peace was disrupted, and flames of wars were lit while the world was full of open deceitfulness, and there was hopelessness.

By God, whatever the Prophet told them, I am here telling you the same, and whatever you hear today is not different from what your elders that passed away had heard. Their eyes were opened for them and their hearts were guided. You are being given the same (message) at this time.

By God, you have not been told anything that they were not told, and you have not been given anything that they were denied. Certainly you have been afflicted by a calamity (trial), so do not let the deceitful people deceive you.
(Sermon 88)

Eulogy of Prophet Muhammad (s)
God sent His prophets successively. They were born of distinguished and chaste lineage. Whenever a prophet died, the next prophet stood up for the cause of the religion of God, until the divine mandate reached Muhammad (s). God brought him out from the same honorable lineage that He brought other prophets.

He is the leader (Imam) of all God-conscious people and a light for those who seek guidance. He is a lamp whose flame is bright. His conduct was upright, his speech (argument) was decisive, and his decision was just. May God shower His Mercy on him.
(Sermon 93)

The Prophet's Low Regard for the Material World:
He treated the vanities of the world disdainfully and had low regard for material things. He removed his heart from worldly desires. He

conveyed God's plea (against committing sins), warned people (against Divine chastisement), and beckoned them towards Paradise and its good tidings.
(Sermon 108)

He Was the Final Prophet:

God deputized the Prophet after a gap of many years after the previous prophets. There was anticipation among the people (of a prophet to come). With him, God concluded the series of prophets sent and concluded His messages.
(Sermon 132)

The Prophet Came to Dissuade People from Idol Worship:

God deputed Muhammad (p) so that he may dissuade His people from the worship of idols and guide them towards the worship of God Almighty. God sent him with His message, the Qur'an, which He taught and explained so that the people may know their sustainer. Through His Book (Qur'an), God revealed (something of) Himself, so that the people would believe in Him even without having seen Him.
(Sermon 146)

Muhammad (s) is an Example to Follow:

Certainly you should follow your Prophet, the pure and the chaste. He is an example to emulate.[1] The most beloved person before God is he who walks in his (Prophet's) footsteps. He enjoyed but little of this world's bounties. He ate less and did not fill his stomach. The world's bounties were offered to him, but he refused them. He disliked what God disliked, and he regarded as lowly what God regarded lowly.

He repaired his own shoes and patched his clothes with his hands. He would ride his animal unsaddled. He detached his heart from this world's attractions and blotted them out from his thoughts. He preferred that the world's allurements should remain away from his

1 "Indeed, there is for you, in the messenger of God (Muhammad), an excellent pattern of conduct" (Qur'an 33:21).

eyes, so that he should not regard this world a place of extended stay.

Certainly, God made Muhammad (s) a conveyor of tidings of Paradise and Warner of His retribution. How great is God's blessing that He sent to us the Prophet, a leader whose example we (aspire to) follow.
(Sermon 159)

A Bright Light and a Clear Argument:
God deputed the Prophet with a bright light, a clear argument, an open path (of righteousness), and a guiding Book (Qur'an). He descended from a noble ancestry, his reputation stood high, and his message spread everywhere. God sent him with a strong plea and a convincing treatise. Through him, God disclosed the ways (of truth) that were forsaken and destroyed the innovations that were introduced. Through him, God explained and clarified His commands.
(Sermon 160)

The Prophet Brought Honor to the People:
Then, God, the Glorified, deputed Muhammad (s) with truth at a time when the destruction of the world seemed near and when its brightness was turning into gloom. The world had become full of trouble for its inhabitants, and its decay had drawn near. God sent him for conveying His message and (a means of) honor for his people, heralding a period of bloom for them, and he was a source of dignity for his supporters and helpers.
(Sermon 197)

Through the Prophet, God United the People of Arabia:
God deputized the Prophet with a light, chose him in preference to others, giving him the highest accord. Through him, God united those who were divided, subdued the powerful. He overcame surmounting difficulties and thereby removed widespread misguidance.
(Sermon 212)

The Noble Lineage of the Prophet (s):

I stand witness that God is just. God chose the line of descent for the Prophet, and no evildoer belonged in his ancestry.[1] God, the Glorified, has granted virtue to those who deserve it, guided them to the truth, and protected them from deviation.

Know that, certainly, those creatures of God who safeguard His knowledge, protect what He desires to be protected, they make divine springs of blessings flow (for the benefit of people). They meet each other with friendliness and affection. They drink water from cups (of knowledge and God-consciousness) that quench the thirst, and they return from the watering places fully satiated. Misgiving does not affect them and backbiting does not appeal to them. God has bestowed them with good manners. They were chosen, just as seeds are selected by keeping some and discarding others. This selection has distinguished them above others and has purified them (the souls). **(Sermon 213)**

---

1 Prophet Muhammad's lineage is traced as follows: Prophet Abraham, Prophet Ishmael, Kedar, Abdul-Muttalib, Abdullah, and then Muhammad. (Peace be upon them all.)

ABOUT OTHER PROPHETS

Introduction: A prophet of God, according to Islamic belief, is an individual deputed by God to represent Him to humanity. He is selected, educated, and trained by God, so that he will deliver God's messages and commands faithfully and truthfully. A Prophet's piety, morals, integrity, and truthfulness are beyond question, and his chastity and conduct are impeccable. Any behavior less than that would make one assume that God made an error in His judgment. There are many named prophets in the Qur'an, but there were many more unnamed prophets sent to humankind. The Arabic names of the prophets given in the Qur'an are different from the Biblical names in the English language.[1] As a Caliph, successor, and confidant to the Prophet Muhammad (s), Imam Ali (p) taught and reinforced reverence and respect for all the earlier prophets of God.

God Chooses His Prophets:

God never allowed His creation to remain without a Prophet of His, or without a Book sent down from Him, or without a binding argument or a plea. These Messengers did not feel overwhelmed by the large number of their opponents or worried by the small number of their supporters. They would name their successors to carry on the message.
(Sermon 1)

About Prophet Moses (p):

I will relate to you concerning Prophet Moses, who conversed with God Almighty. He said:

---

1 Please refer to the appendix for details.

"O God! I need whatever good You may grant me." **(Qur'an 28:24)**

By God, he asked only for bread to eat, because he was eating the herbs of the earth, and the greenness of the herbs could be seen from his skin.
(Sermon 159)

About Prophet David (p):
I can give you another example, that of Prophet David (p). He was the reciter of the Psalms. He made baskets from palm leaves with his own hands and would ask his companions if they would buy them. He used to eat barley bread purchased from his earnings.
(Sermon 159)

About Prophet Jesus (p):
I will tell you about Jesus, the son of Mary. He used a stone for his pillow, put on coarse clothes, ate simple food, and preferred to go hungry. His lamp at night was the moon. His covering during the winter was just the expanse of earth. His fruits were those that grow naturally in the wilderness that are eaten by cattle. He had no wife to comfort him, nor a son, nor wealth to distract him, nor did he have greed (for worldly things). His two feet were the sole means of his transportation, and his two hands were his servants.
(Sermon 159)

About the Deniers of the Prophets of God;
Praise be to God, the Exalted and Most High, who chose His Prophets in preference to the rest of His creation. The rejecters and deniers of His prophets deserve His wrath.
(Sermon 191)

Moses (p), son of Imran (Amran), went to Pharaoh along with his brother Aaron, wearing (coarse) clothes of wool and holding sticks in their hands, guaranteeing Pharaoh his throne and honor if only he submitted to God. However, Pharaoh said to his people, "Do you not wonder at these two men guaranteeing me the continuity of my honor and the retention of my country, although you see their poverty and lowliness? Why do they not have gold bangles on their wrists?" Pharaoh felt proud of his wealth and looked down upon the (coarse) woolen clothes of Moses (p).[1]

If God had desired for His prophets, He would have granted them treasures of gold and surrounded them with beautiful gardens. If He had done so, then there would have been no trial for the people, nor any recompense (in the next world). However, God, the Glorified, sends them as ordinary-looking people, appearing contemptible to the eyes of the disbelievers.

If the Prophets possessed authority and honor, then it would be very easy for people to believe in them and they would acknowledge them out of fear. Therefore, God decided that people should follow His prophets, acknowledge His books, remain humble to Him, and obey His commands with sincerity, without an iota of other motives (i.e., fear and greed).

(Sermon 191)

1 Pharaoh said to his people, "Nay, am I not better than this fellow (Moses), who is contemptible, scarcely capable of speaking distinctly? Why have no bracelets of gold been put upon him?" (Qur'an Chapter 43:52, 53)

IMAM ALI (P) ABOUT HIMSELF

Introduction: Much has been written about Imam Ali (p) by Muslim and non-Muslim scholars and historians. *Ibn Abil Hadid,*[1] the well-known Egyptian commentator of the book "*Nahjul Balagha,*" states:

"Ali had a personality in which opposing characteristics had so gathered themselves that it was difficult to believe that such a combination could manifest itself in a human being. He was the bravest man and the boldest warrior that history could cite, and while such brave persons are hard-hearted, cruel, and bloodthirsty, instead, Ali was kind, sympathetic, responsive, and a warm-hearted person. These are the qualities of the God-fearing. He was friendly with the rich, the poor, the educated, and the ignorant alike. He had a tender spot in his heart for every downtrodden, crippled, widowed, and orphaned person."

Presented in this chapter are excerpts of the Imam's sayings and guidance to the Muslims clarifying his position on many issues.

Imam Ali (p) Explains His Position:
O God! I am the first who leaned (towards Thee) and who heard and responded (to the call to submission). No one preceded me in offering (ritual) prayers except the Prophet (s).

1 Ibn Abil Hadid has written an extensive commentary covering several volumes on Imam Ali's book *Nahjul Balagha*. It is in the Arabic language.

The Scope of His Knowledge:

One of the Imam's companions said to him: "O Amir-ul-Mu'mineen, you have been given knowledge of hidden things." Whereupon, Imam Ali laughed and said to the man:

"O brother, this is not knowledge of hidden things. This knowledge I have acquired from the Prophet. As regards the knowledge of hidden things, that means knowledge of the Day of Judgment and the things covered by God as stated in the following verse:

'Verily, God is He with Whom is the knowledge of the Hour' **[Qur'an 31:34].**

"Therefore, God alone knows what is there in the wombs, whether male or female, ugly or handsome, generous or miserly, mischievous or pious, and who will be doomed to Hell and who will be in the company of the Prophets in Paradise. This is the knowledge of the hidden things, which is not known to anyone save God. God transmitted all other knowledge to the Prophet Muhammad (s), who then passed it to me. He prayed to God that my bosom may retain this knowledge."
(Sermon 127)

His Prophecy about the Future:

Certainly a time will come after I leave, when nothing will be more disliked than virtue, and nothing more liked than vice.
(Sermon 146)

About His Knowledge:

By God, I can tell every one of you where you have come from, or where you have to go. I can tell you about your affairs, but I fear lest you abandon the Messenger of God in my favor. I shall certainly convey these things to the selected ones, who will remain safe from being misguided. By God, Who deputed the Prophet with truth and distinguished him over all creation, I do not speak save the truth.
(Sermon 174)

O people! Ask me before you lose me, because certainly I am even more acquainted with the paths of the heavens than the paths of the earth. **(Sermon 188)**

About His Status and His Contributions to Islam:
Certainly if God were to allow anyone to indulge in pride, He would have allowed it to his selected prophets and vicegerents. However, God, the Sublime, disliked vanity for them and preferred humility for them. Therefore, they remained humble. God tried them with hunger, afflicted them with difficulty, tested them with fear, and upset them with troubles. Therefore, do not regard wealth and progeny as the criterion for God's pleasure and displeasure. You are not aware of the mischief and trials that wealth and power bring. God, the Glorified, the Sublime, has said:

"What! Do they think that (by) what We aid them with of wealth and children, We are hastening unto them the good things? Nay! They perceive not"[1] (**Qur'an 23:55–56**).

Certainly God, the Glorified, tries His subjects, who are vain, by making His beloved subjects appear lowly to them.

God, the Glorified, if He wished, He could open for His Prophets treasures and mines of gold and plant gardens for them. If He had done so, then there would have been no trial, nor recompense, nor any good tidings (to the people for their obedience).

God, the Glorified, decided that people should follow His prophets, acknowledge His books, remain humble before Him, obey His command, and accept His obedience without an iota of any other motive except sincerity.

God tries His creatures through difficulties and expects them to worship Him even in hardship. He causes them distresses in order to

1 Meaning, wealth, and offspring are a trial and may corrupt a person and cause him/her to fall into temptations.

remove vanity from their hearts, and then He opens the door of His favors and forgiveness.

Satan felt proud because of his origin from fire and taunted Adam about his origin from clay. In the same way, the rich feel vain because of their riches, as (God) said:

"And said they: 'We are more (than you) in wealth and in children, and we shall not be chastised!'" **[Qur'an 34:35].**

In case you cannot avoid vanity, then take pride in performing good acts, like helping a neighbor, the fulfillment of contracts, extending generosity to others, keeping away from bloodshed, doing justice to people, and suppressing anger. You should also keep in mind what happened to the people before you, and be careful that you do not make the same mistakes.

Think about the condition of people from among the believers who passed away long ago. The Pharaohs took them as slaves. They inflicted on them the worst punishments and bitter sufferings. They remained in this state of ruinous disgrace and severe subjugation. They found no method for escape and no protection. God, the Glorified, knowing that they were enduring troubles in His love and bearing distresses for His sake, provided them escape from their distress and trials. He changed their disgrace into honor and fear into safety. Consequently, they became rulers, kings, and leaders, and God's favors over them were beyond their expectations.

See what happened to them towards the end, when divisions overtook them and their unity was fractured. There were differences in what they said and what was actually in their hearts. They broke into groups and were scattered. They fought among themselves. Then God took away from them the apparel of His honor and deprived them of their prosperity. Their stories have remained among you for those who may take lesson.

Beware! You let go the obedience and you have again reverted to the manners of the Bedouin Arabs, breaking into different parties after having been united.

Beware! Surely God has commanded me to fight those who revolt or who break the pledge or create trouble on the earth. As regards the pledge breakers, I have fought them; as regards to the deviators from the truth, I have waged war against them; and as regards to those who have rebelled and gone out of the faith, I have disgraced them.

Even in my young age, I had subdued (famous warriors). Certainly you know my close kinship and special relationship with the Prophet of God. He found no untruth in my speech nor weakness in my actions.

I used to follow him like a young camel following its mother. Every day he would show me some of his high traits and command me to follow them. Every year he used to go in seclusion to the *cave of Hira,*[1] where I was with him alone. In those days, Islam did not exist in any house except that of the Prophet of God and Khadijah (His wife), while I was the third person after these two to be blessed with Islam. I used to watch the effulgence of Divine revelations and messages as they descended upon the Prophet.

When the revelation descended on the Prophet of God, I heard the moan of Satan. I asked, "O Prophet of God, what is this moan?" and he replied, "This is Satan, who has lost all hope of being worshipped. O Ali, you see all that I see and you hear all that I hear, except that you are not a Prophet, but you are a vicegerent and you are surely on (the path of) virtue."

Certainly I belong to the group of people who care not for the reproach of anyone in matters concerning God. Their countenance is the countenance of the truthful, and their speech is the speech of the

1 In the cave on top of mountain near Mecca where the Prophet (s) received his first revelation brought by Angel Gabriel.

virtuous. They are wakeful during the nights (in devotion to God) and are beacons (of guidance) in the day. They hold fast to (teachings of) the Qur'an and revive the traditions of God and of His Prophet. They do not boast nor indulge in self-conceit, nor misappropriate, nor create mischief. Their hearts are in Paradise while their bodies (on earth) are busy (in good acts).
(Sermon 191)

His Reliance upon God:
Surely God has provided a strong protective shield over me. When my time to depart comes, it (the shield) will be removed from me, and death will overtake me.
(Sermon 61)

About His Forbearance:
I lived as a good neighbor to you and tried my best to look after you, and I freed you from the snare of humility and the fetters of oppression. I closed my eyes to many misdeeds that you committed.
(Sermon 158)

His Austere Lifestyle and Abstinence from the World's Allurements
By God, I have been sewing so many patches on my shirt that now I feel embarrassed of it.
(Sermon 159)

O world! Do not try to snare me, for I am above your temptations, and I carefully avoid pitfalls. Where are those people whom you had tempted with pleasures and enjoyments? Where are those groups whom you had allured with pomp and glory? They are now in their graves under tons of earth.

O world! Had you been a person or a being with life and limbs, I would have punished you under the laws of the Lord. Because, you have tempted (and misguided) millions of individuals from the true path of humanity, you have given them false hopes, brought about their destruction, caused the decline and fall of nations, and allured them with power and pleasures.

O world, Woe to the man who, with misplaced confidence, steps on your slippery surface; you made it to appear as a firm foothold, for he will certainly slip (get misguided); woe to the man who is tempted to ride the waves of false hopes and (unrealistic) expectations raised by you, for he will surely sink.

Whoever avoids your trap, your temptations, your snares, and your allurements, he will find the straight path to safety and salvation. Whoever rejects you, he does not care for the consequences of his action, even though he may find himself in difficulties. The life of this world with its pleasures and afflictions is like a day that will soon pass away. Leave me alone, you cannot catch me unawares in order to plunge me into disgrace and humiliation.

I swear by God, barring Destiny over which I have no control, that I shall exert self-control so that I shall be contented and happy, even if I have one piece of bread with a pinch of salt, and that I will keep my heart free from desire for power, pleasure, and glory.
(Letter 45)

When a Man Offered Him a Gift:

A man came and offered me a flask full of honey, but I was disinclined to accept it. I asked him whether it was a reward or charity, for these are forbidden to us, the members of the Prophet's family. He said it was a gift. Then I said, "Have you come to seduce me away from the religion of God?" [i.e., Imam could sense that the person's motive was to ask for some undue favor in return].

By God, even if I am given all the domain of the (seven) heavens, with all that exists under the skies, in order that I may disobey God to the extent of snatching one grain of barley from an ant, I would not do it. For me, all the (riches of the) world are (worth) less than the leaf in the mouth of a locust that it is chewing. What has Ali to do with bounties that will pass away, and from the evil (consequences) of mistakes, and from Him we seek succor.

(Sermon 222)

His Sermon Shortly Before His Death:

O people! Everyone has to meet death; life is leading everyone to it. The knowledge of the time of death is hidden. I testify that I do not believe in a partner for God, and I do not disregard the teachings of Muhammad (s). Therefore, (I advise you) to be attached to these two pillars and keep lighted these two lamps. If you stay undivided, no evil will come to you. Each one of you has to bear your own burden. God is Merciful. Faith is straightforward. The leader (Prophet) is the holder of knowledge. Yesterday I was with you, today I have become the object of a lesson for you, and tomorrow I shall leave you. May God forgive you and me?

I was your neighbor and gave you company, but shortly you will find me lifeless. The stillness of my limbs may provide you counsel, because it is a more effective counsel than an eloquent speech. I am departing from you like one who is eager to meet (God). Tomorrow, you will look back at my services, then my inner side (valuable and sincere services) will come to your attention, and you will realize that better after another individual takes my place.

(Sermon 148)

Advice to His Family Before Dying:

My advice to you is that you should not consider anyone as equal to the Lord; be firm in your belief that there is One and only One God. Do not waste the knowledge given to you by the Prophet (s), and do not forego or lose his teachings (traditions). Keep these two pillars of Islam aloft. If you act according to my advice, then you cannot be blamed for corrupting the religion.

Until yesterday, I was your leader; today I am only an object from whom you can take lesson and warnings, and tomorrow I shall part company with you. If I survive this wound, I shall be at liberty to de-

cide how to deal with the man who attempted to kill me. If I die, then my worldly life will end. If I forgive my assassin, it will be to gain the blessings of God for forgiving him, who has harmed me. It will be a good deed if you also forgive him. Do you not desire to be forgiven by the Lord? As far as death by martyrdom is concerned, I always anticipated and desired it, and I now welcome it like a very thirsty person who finds water. I am a seeker who finds what he was seeking (i.e., martyrdom). The pious people will receive the best from God.
(Letter 23)

A Statement of the Prophet (s) to Imam Ali (p)

"O Ali, no faithful Muslim will ever be your enemy and no hypocrite will ever be your friend."

ABOUT THE FAMILY OF MUHAMMAD (S)

Introduction: The family of Prophet Muhammad (s) is blessed with an exalted and honored position in Islam. His daughter, Fatima (p), his cousin and son-in-Law, Ali (p), and his grandsons, Hasan and Husain (pp), were not only very special to him, but also blessed and purified from all sins and faults. There are several verses in the Qur'an in their praise. The designated Imams from his family were the spiritual leaders of the Muslims. Their God-consciousness was unmatched, and their knowledge of the Qur'an was next only to that of the Prophet (s).

About the (Chosen) Members of the Family of the Prophet: They are the trustees of God's secrets, shelter for His affairs, source of knowledge about Him, center of His wisdom, valleys for His books, and (lofty) mountains of His religion. With them, God straightened the bend in religion's back and removed the trembling in its limbs.
(Sermon 2)

Beware! The example of the descendants of Muhammad (s) is like that of stars in the sky. When one star sets, another one rises. Therefore, you are in a position that God's blessings on you have been perfected.
(Sermon 99)

We (the chosen members) are the tree of prophethood, the resting place of the (Divine) Message, descending place of angels, the mines of knowledge, and the source of wisdom. Our supporters and lovers await mercy while our enemy awaits wrath (of God).
(Sermon 108)

About the Descendants of the Prophet (s):
The chosen members of his family are the reins of righteousness, ensigns of faith, and tongues of truth. You should accord to them the same high position that you accord to the Qur'an, and come to them (for quenching the thirst for guidance) as the thirsty camels approach the water spring.
(Sermon 86)

To Follow in the Footsteps of the Family of the Prophet (s):
Look up to the members of the Prophet's family. Adhere to the direction they guide you. Follow their footsteps, because they would never let you go astray. If they sit down, you sit down, and if they rise up, you rise up. Do not try to precede them, as you would thereby go astray, and do not lag behind them, as you would thereby be ruined.
(Sermon 96)

About the Greatness of the Members of the Prophet's Family:
By God, I have knowledge of the conveyance of messages and fulfillment of the promises. We, the people of the House (of the Prophet), possess the doors of wisdom and light of governance. The path of religion is one and its highway is straight. He who stood away from it went astray.
(Sermon 119)

Prophet's Family Members Endowed with Knowledge:
Where are those who falsely claimed that they were deeply versed in knowledge! God had raised us in position and kept them down, bestowed upon us knowledge but deprived them of it. With us, the blindness (of misguidance) is to be changed into brightness of guidance. Surely the Imams (divinely appointed leaders) will be from the Quresh tribe.

Imam Ali (p) Responding to Those Who Challenged His Status and Authority:
Where are the hearts dedicated and devoted to the obedience of God? They are all crowding towards worldly vanities and quarrelling

over unlawful issues. They have turned their faces away from Paradise. God called them, but they turned away. When Satan called them, they responded.
(Sermon 143)

They Speak the Truth and are Treasurers of God:
He who has an intelligent mind looks to his goal. He knows his low road as well as his high road.

They (the opponents of the Prophet's family) have entered the oceans of disturbance and have taken to innovations instead of the Sunnah (the Prophet's teachings and practices). While the believers are subdued, the misguided and the falsifiers are vocal. We are the near ones (to God), treasure holders and doors (to the teachings of the Prophet). Houses are not entered save through the doors. Whoever enters from other than the door is called a thief. (The implied meaning here is that to receive true knowledge, approach the chosen members of the family of the Prophet).

They are the treasurers of God. When they speak, they speak the truth, but when they keep silent, no one else speaks for them (i.e., no one has anything better to say).
(Sermon 153)

About the Knowledge of the Family of the Prophet:
They are "life" for knowledge and "death" for ignorance. Their forbearance tells you about their knowledge, and their silence indicates their wisdom. Neither do they go against what is right, nor do they differ (among themselves) about it. They are the pillars of faith and its protectors. With them, truth has returned to its proper place and wrong has been uprooted. They have understood the religion, not by mere hearsay or from relaters. The relaters of knowledge are many, but only a few understand it.
(Sermon 237)

We, the chosen from the family of the Holy Prophet, hold such a central and pivotal position in religion that those who are seeking an understanding of principles and practice of the religion will have to come to us for help (and guidance).
(A Saying)

The Knower of the Rights of the Prophet and His Family:
Any one of you who dies (a natural death), while he/she has knowledge of the rights of God and the rights of His Prophet and the rights of the (chosen) members of his family will die the death of a martyr (in the service of God). His/her reward is incumbent upon God.
(Sermon 189)

ABOUT ISLAM

Introduction: The Arabic word *Islam* means peace and submission. In the religious sense, in principle, it is professing that there is no god but God, and Muhammad (s) is the Messenger of God. In a practical sense, it is submission to the Will of God. For a Muslim, it requires belief in one God, belief in all the previous prophets of God, following the teachings of Muhammad (s), and obeying the commands (laws) contained in the Qur'an. In this chapter, Imam Ali (p) presents his perspective regarding his religious beliefs, his strong faith in God, and his belief in the prophethood of Muhammad (s).

He Defines Islam:
I shall define Islam for you in a way that nobody has done before me.

Islam means obedience to God. Obedience to God means having sincere faith in Him. Such a faith means to believe in His Power. Belief in His Power means recognizing and accepting His Majesty. Acceptance of His Majesty means fulfilling the obligations laid down. The fulfillment of obligations means actions. (Therefore, Islam does not mean mere faith, but it is faith accompanied with action).
(His saying)

He Explains the Merits of Islam:
Praise be to God who established Islam and made it easy for those who approach it and gave strength to it against anyone who tries to overpower it. Therefore, God made it (a source of) peace for him who attaches to it, safety for him who enters it, argument for him who speaks about it, witness for him who fights (in defense) with its

help. He made it a (source of) light for him who seeks light from it, a means of understanding for him who supports it, a source of sagacity for him who strives, and a sign (of guidance) for him who is receptive. He made it a lesson for him who seeks advice, a means of salvation for him who testifies, a source of confidence for him who trusts, a surety for him who relies, and a shield for him who endures.

It is the brightest of all the paths and clearest of all passages. It has bright highways, burning lamps, prestigious fields of activity, and high objectives. It is sought after earnestly. Its observers are honorable, the testimony (to oneness of God) is its way, and good deeds are its high points.
(Sermon 105)

Addressing the Misguided Followers of Islam:
God is bounteous to you, for you have acquired a position where even your servants are honored and your neighbors are treated well. However, now you see pledges to God being broken, but you do not feel enraged, although you fret and frown on the breaking of the traditions of your ancestors. You have preferred the company of deviators and delegated your affairs in their hands. They have doubts in what they do and they act in pursuit of their (selfish) desires. God will gather you all on a day (Day of Reckoning) that would be hard on the wrongdoers.
(Sermon 105)

Means of Seeking Nearness to God:
The best means to seek nearness to God is to believe in Him (His Oneness) and His Prophet and fight to defend His cause, for it is the highest pinnacle of faith. It is to believe in His (God's) purity and justice; to establish (ritual) prayers, for they are the foundation of the community; to pay the poor-due (Islamic charity or *Zakaat*), for it is an obligation; to fast for one month in the month of Ramadan, for it is a shield against chastisement; to perform Hajj (Pilgrimage) to the House of God (K 'aba), for it drives away poverty and washes away sins.

Also, to have regard for kinship, for it increases wealth and increases the length of life (as a reward from God); to give alms secretly, for it covers shortcomings; to give alms openly, for it protects against a bad death, and to be of benefit (to people), for it protects from falling into disgrace.

Keep God in remembrance, for it is the best remembrance, and desire for that which He has promised to the pious people, for His promise is the truest promise. Adopt the way of the Prophet, for that is the most distinguished way. Follow the teaching and practice of the Prophet, for it is the most honorable of all practices.

Learn the Qur'an, for it is the fairest of discourses, and understand it thoroughly, for it is the best for blossoming of hearts. Seek cure with its light, for it is cure for (the ailments of) hearts. Recite it beautifully, for it is the most beautiful narration.

Certainly a scholar who acts not according to his knowledge is like the off-headed ignorant who does not find relief from his ignorance. On the learned, the plea of God is greater, grief incumbent, and he is more blameworthy before God for his faults.
(Sermon 109)

God Chose Islam[1] (Submission to God)

This Islam is the religion that God has chosen for Himself, developed it before His eyes, preferred it as the best among His creations and established its pillars on His love. He has given honor to it above other creeds. He has humbled its enemies and frustrated its opponents by giving His support. He has smashed the pillars of misguidance with it. He has quenched the thirst of the thirsty from its cisterns.

He made Islam such that its constituent parts cannot break up: Its links cannot separate. Its structure cannot fall. Its columns cannot decay, and it cannot be uprooted. In addition, its time does not end: Its laws do

1 In the Qur'an, the Prophet Abraham is referred to as Muslim, i.e., he submitted to the Will of God. .

not expire. Its paths do not become narrow. Its ease does not change into difficulty. Its clarity is not affected by gloom. Its straightness does not become crooked. Its vast paths have no narrowness. Its lamp cannot be put out, and its sweetness does not change to bitterness.

Its foundation is strong and built on truthfulness. Its streams are ever full. Its lamps remain ever lighted, and its beacons help travelers seeking guidance. God has granted Islam His highest pleasure: Made it the pinnacle of His pillars and the path to His obedience. Therefore, you should honor it and follow it. Fulfill its obligations and accord it the position it deserves.

Then, God, the Glorified, deputed Muhammad (s) with the message of truth, at a time when the brightness of civilization was turning into gloom. The world had become troublesome for its inhabitants, and its decay had approached near. God made him responsible for conveying His message and made it (a means of) honor for his people, a source of dignity for its supporters, and an honor for his helpers.
(Sermon 197)

ABOUT THE QUR'AN

(Known as "Koran" in the West)

Introduction: The divinely revealed scripture to Prophet Muhammad (s) is unique among all scriptures. The Angel Gabriel brought the messages from God to Muhammad (s). The revelations continued over a period of twenty-three years. Muhammad repeated the messages (verses or chapter) to his disciples, who memorized them. The revelations were also inscribed on parchments. Nonetheless, generation after generation, Muslims continue to memorize the entire scripture word for word. The written word of God in Arabic in the Qur'an is exactly same as it was memorized and inscribed from the time it was revealed to the Prophet. Therefore, the authenticity of the scripture as the original word of God is preserved beyond any doubt. Not only the language of the revelation is alive and current, but also the message is as relevant today as it was 1,400 years ago. In this chapter, Imam Ali (p) expounds on some of the spiritual aspects of the Qur'an.[1]

The Contents of the Qur'an:

The Prophet (s) left for you the Book (Qur'an), which clarifies the permitted and the prohibited by God, the obligatory and the discretionary. It contains topics that are general as well as particular; it has lessons and illustrations, and long and short verses. There are verses whose knowledge is obligatory.

(Sermon 1)

---

1 For more information on the topic of the Qur'an, please visit **www.islamquery.com**.

God Says in the Qur'an:

"We have not neglected anything in the Book (Qur'an)." **(Qur'an 6:38)**

The Qur'an is Free of any Discrepancies:

"And if it had been from any other than God, they would surely have found in it much discrepancy."

(Qur'an 4:82)[2]

(Sermon 18)

The Apparent and the Hidden in the Qur'an:

Certainly, the outside of the Qur'an (exoteric) is wonderful, and its inside is deep (in meaning). Its wonders will never end, its amazements will never exhaust, and its intricacies cannot be comprehended, except through itself.

The Qur'an, a Fair Discourse:

Learn the Qur'an, for it is the fairest of discourses, and (strive to) understand it thoroughly, for it is the best for blossoming of hearts. Seek cure with its light, for it is the cure for (the diseases of) the hearts. Recite it in a beautiful manner, for it is the most beautiful of all narrations.

(Sermon 109)

Qur'an is a "House with Sturdy Pillars":

The Book of God is among you. It speaks and its tongue does not falter. It is a house, whose supports do not crumble and a power whose helpers cannot be routed.

(Sermon 132)

---

2 This refers to the revelations that came over a span of twenty-three years of the ministry of Prophet Muhammad (s). There is no contradiction in the messages, despite such a long period of revelations. This itself is a proof that Qur'an is a Divine revelation. If it were a "man-made" book, as alleged by the opponents, then contradictions would be unavoidable.

Qur'an is a "Lamp":
Its wonders are inexhaustible and its subtleties are unending. It is a light (of guidance) for the darkness (of ignorance). (The doors of) virtue cannot be opened save with its keys, nor can gloom be dispelled save with its light. God has protected its inaccessible points (from enemies) and allowed grazing (to its followers) in its pastures. It contains the remedy (for the ailment of misguidance) for the seeker.
(Sermon 151)

Qur'an is a "Strong Rope":
The Qur'an is a strong rope, a clear light, a cure, a quencher for thirst (for knowledge), a protector and deliverer (from calamities). Therefore, I advise you to adhere to it. There is no crookedness in it. Hearing its repeated recitation does not fatigue the ears. Quoting the Qur'an is expounding the truth.
(Sermon 155)

Qur'an Contains Knowledge of the Future:
The Prophet came with a Book (Qur'an) testifying to the (older) Scriptures. It contains knowledge of what is to come about in the future, the stories of the past, cure for your (spiritual and moral) ills, and regulations for all the situations that you might face.
(Sermon 157)

Qur'an is an Advisor:
The Qur'an is an advisor, a leader that never deceives, and a narrator that never speaks a lie. No one will sit (listen or recite) beside this Qur'an but that when he rises up, he will achieve either guidance or healing of (spiritual) blindness. You should know that no one will need any other guidance after (receiving guidance from) the Qur'an. Therefore, seek cure from it for your ailments, and seek its assistance in your distress. It contains a cure for the worst of the diseases, including the unbelief (in God), hypocrisy, rebellion (against God), and misguidance (from the true Path). Pray to God through its recitation and turn to God with its help. There is nothing like the Qur'an, through which one should turn to God, the Sublime.

Know that the Qur'an is an (effective) intercessor[1] and its intercession will be accepted (on the Day of Reckoning). Therefore, you should be among the adherents and followers of the Qur'an.

Make it your guide for seeking God. Follow its advice and do not rely on your own views beyond what is in the Qur'an.

God, the Glorified, has not counseled anyone with the likes of this Qur'an, for it is the strong rope (support) of God and His trustworthy means. It contains the blossoming of the heart and springs of knowledge. For the heart, there is no other purifier better than the Qur'an.
(Sermon 175)

Qur'an is Proof of God:

The Qur'an orders as well as refrains, and it remains silent as well as speaks. It is the proof of God for His creation. He has perfected its effulgence and has perfected His religion through it. He deputed the Prophet to convey to the people all His commands through it.
(Sermon 182)

Qur'an is the Quencher of Thirst for the Seeker of Knowledge:

Then God sent to the Prophet (s) the Book (Qur'an) as a lamp whose flame cannot be extinguished, a light whose brightness does not diminish, a sea whose depth cannot be fathomed, a way that does not mislead, and a ray of light that does not dim. It is a discriminator (of good from evil) whose arguments cannot not be belittled, a clarifier whose foundation cannot be shaken, a cure which leaves no trace of the disease, a book of honor whose supporters cannot be overcome, and a truth whose helpers are not abandoned. It is the mine of belief, the

1 This term implies that on the Day of Judgment, those who recited the Qur'an, pondered over its meaning, and obeyed its commandments will receive forgiveness and due rewards.

source of knowledge, the courtyard of justice, the foundation stone of Islam, the valleys and the plains of truth, the spring whose water is inexhaustible, the goal that the travelers striving towards it do not get lost, and the signpost that no seeker fails to see.

God has made it a quencher of the thirst of the learned, a blooming for the hearts of religious jurists, a highway for the ways of the righteous, a cure after which no ailment remains, a brightness with which no darkness remains, a rope whose grip is strong, a fortress that is invulnerable. It honors him who loves it, a place of peace for him who enters it, a guide for him who follows it, a success for him who argues with its help, a witness against him who rebukes it. It is a shield for him who arms himself (against misguidance), a source of knowledge for him who listens to it carefully, a worthy narration for him who recites it, and a conclusive verdict for him who gives out judgment (according to it).

(Sermon 197)

K'ABA (THE HOUSE OF GOD) AND THE HAJJ PILGRIMAGE

Introduction: The K'aba is the symbolic House of God on earth, situated in Mecca (in present-day Saudi Arabia). It is approximately a fifty-foot-by-fifty-foot-by-fifty-foot cubicle, originally built by the first man on Earth, the Prophet Adam (p), according to Divine instructions for the worship of God Almighty. It was rebuilt by the Prophet Abraham (p), father of the three monotheistic religions—Judaism, Christianity, and Islam—with the help of his son Ishmael (p). It was rebuilt again in the time of Muhammad (s), the last prophet of God. Muslims are required to perform the pilgrimage to the K'aba once in their lifetime as an obligatory duty. This takes place in the twelfth month of the Muslim calendar, the month of *Dhul Hijjah*. Millions of believers from around the world perform the pilgrimage (Hajj) every year.

Imam Ali (p) here reminds the pilgrims that visiting this place during Hajj should be purely for the pleasure of God and devoid of worldly motives. Moreover, he notes that hardships encountered during the journey are a test of faith.

God's Divine Plan with Regard to His House, the K'aba: God, the Glorified, had made His sacred house (Ka'ba) in the most rugged part of the earth, in a narrow valley between rough mountains (in the city of Mecca). At that time, the arid desert and scanty water resources allowed neither camels nor horses nor cows nor sheep to prosper.

Then He commanded the Prophet Adam and his sons to attend to it. In this way, it became the focus of their journeys. Since that time, human beings have hastened towards it from distant lands, traveling through waterless deserts, deep and low-lying valleys, and scattered islands. They arrive in humility, reciting the slogan of having reached the audience of God Almighty, hurrying on foot with disheveled appearance and dust-covered faces. They are required to stay unshaven during the rituals as a means of trial. God has made it a condition to His mercy and an approach to His Paradise.

If God, the Glorified, had placed His sacred House and His great signs among lush plantations, streams of water, soft and level plains, abundance of trees, a flourishing population, and laden orchards, then the amount of spiritual recompense to the pilgrims would have decreased because of the lightness of the trial. If the House were built with green emeralds and red rubies, then this would have lessened the doubts in people's minds (i.e., they would be readily attracted toward it), and it would have decreased Satan's evil influence on the hearts (i.e., in discouraging people from journeying to the house of God). However, God tries His subjects by means of various difficulties, and wants them to worship Him despite hardships and distresses. He wishes to remove vanity from their hearts, to induce humility in their spirits, and thereby open the doors of His favors, bounties, and forgiveness.
(Sermon 191)

Imam Ali's Saying about Hajj Pilgrimage:
God has made obligatory upon you the pilgrimage (Hajj) to His sacred house (K'aba), which is the direction towards which people turn their faces (while performing ritual worship) and proceed towards it (K'aba) like the beasts or pigeons that go towards the water spring[1] (to quench thirst). God, the Glorified, made it a sign of their submission to His Greatness and their acknowledgement of His Exalted status. He chose (humankind) from among His creation, so that, on

1 The implied meaning is that people go on Hajj pilgrimage to the House of God to quench their thirst for seeking nearness to God (spiritual thirst).

listening to His call, they would respond to it, and would honor His command. They thus responded and resembled His angels who surround the Divine Throne (located in the higher Heaven), securing all the benefits of performing His worship, and hastening towards His promised forgiveness. God, the Glorified, made it (His sacred house) an emblem for Islam and an object of respect for those who turn to it. He made obligatory its pilgrimage and laid down its claim, for which He held you responsible to discharge. Thus, God, the Glorified, said:

"And pilgrimage to the house is incumbent upon humankind for the sake of God, (upon) everyone who is able to undertake the journey to it; and whoever disbelieves (in it), then surely God is Self-Sufficient, above any need of the worlds." **(Qur'an 3:96)**
(Sermon 1)

ISLAMIC RITUAL PRAYERS (*SALAAT*)

Introduction: The ritual prayer in Islam is called *Salaat* in Arabic. It is an obligation that is required to be performed five times a day and is one of the "Pillars" of Islam. In this Chapter, by employing rich analogies, Imam Ali (p) emphatically and eloquently illuminates the importance of *Salaat.*

Pledge yourself with Salaat (ritual prayers) and remain steady on it. Offer (optional) prayers as much as possible (in addition to the obligatory prayers) and seek nearness (to God) through them. It is (ordained) upon the believers as a timed ordinance.

Have you not heard the reply of the people of Hell when they were asked:

"What hath brought you into the hell?' They shall say: 'We were not of those who prayed (to God).'" **(Qur'an 74:42–43)**

Certainly prayer sheds sins like the shedding of leaves (from trees in fall). The Messenger of God has likened it to a warm bath, easily accessible to a person who bathes in it five times a day. (He asked,) Will then any dirt remain on him?

This obligation is well recognized by those believers whom neither wealth nor children can turn away from it. God, the Glorified, says:

"Men whom neither merchandise nor any sale diverts from the remembrance of God, and constancy in prayer and paying the charity (Zakat)."[1] **(Qur'an 24:7)**

Even after receiving assurance of Paradise, the Messenger of God (s) used to exert himself to perform prayers, because of the command of God, the Glorified:

"And enjoin prayer on thy followers, and adhere thou steadily unto it." **(Qur'an 20:32)**

The Prophet used to enjoin prayers on his followers and he himself exerted considerably in them.
(Sermon 198)

---

1 The Islamic charity (*Zakat*) is laid down along with ritual prayers as a sacrifice and obligation to be carried out by the Muslims. Whoever pays the *Zakat* by way of purifying his soul (and monies), it serves as a purifier for him and a protection and shield against fire (of Hell). No one, therefore, should miss it or have regrets. Whoever pays it without the intention of purifying his heart is ill informed of the teachings of the Prophet (s). He may forfeit the reward for it. His act is compromised and may need atonement.

ABOUT SATAN

Introduction: Satan, Jinn by origin, is a very interesting character. The Qur'an has many references to him. His proper name in Arabic is *Iblees (Lucifer in English),* but he is more commonly known as *Shaytaan.* When he disobeyed God by refusing to prostrate himself before the Prophet Adam while all the angels prostrated themselves. God asked Satan why he refused to prostrate himself. Satan said that he was superior to Adam because he was created from fire, whereas Adam was created from lowly clay. God called him vain and rejected him (from God's favor). He left Paradise promising that he would seduce and make humans go astray from the Right Path (i.e., the way of obedience to God). God responded by saying that those who follow Satan will be punished along with the accursed *Jinn.* Thus, Satan afflicts humans by causing them to feel vain and superior to others. This includes a feeling of superiority in respect to wealth, race, color, family heritage, country of origin, language, ethnicity, etc. In this manner, Satan recruits humankind to his flock and shepherds them to doom and punishment.

In this chapter, Imam Ali (p) points out various types of traps and tools of deception that Satan uses to misguide people and ruin their Hereafter.

A Warning against Satan:

I enjoin upon you to be God-conscious, for He has left no excuse against what He has warned and has exhausted arguments (of guidance) about the (right) path that He has shown. He has warned you

of the enemy (Satan) that sneaks into hearts and stealthily prompts, and thereby misguides, bringing about destruction. He makes (false) promises and practices deception. He presents evil and sin in attractive shapes and appearances and makes major transgressions (against God) appear minor.
(Sermon 82)

Satan Promised to Lead People Astray:
Therefore, you should fear lest Satan infect you with his disease, or lead you astray through his call, because, by my life, he has put the arrow (of deception) in the bow for you, has stretched the bow strongly, and has aimed it at you from a nearby position. As stated in the Qur'an, this is what Satan promised to God,

"He said: 'My Lord! Because Thou hast left me to stray, certainly will I adorn unto them (the humankind) the path of error, and certainly will I cause them all to go astray' " (Qur'an 15:39).

He (Satan) had said so, only by conjecture about the future that was unknown to him. However, the sons of vanity, the brothers of haughtiness, and the knights of pride and intolerance proved him to be true, so much so that when disobedient persons bowed before him (Satan) and his sway gathered strength, he gained full control (over his victims) using the forces under his command.
(Sermon 191)

ABOUT DIVISIVENESS

Introduction: Maintaining peace, harmony, and unity in the community has been greatly emphasized in Islam, in the Qur'an, and in the teachings of Prophet Muhammad (s). If a person helps make peace between two parties or makes up with an estranged relative or friend, then he earns the pleasure of God and a reward greater than many acts of worship. Imam Ali (p) showed a great amount of magnanimity and self-sacrifice as a ruler by forgiving his adversaries in order to maintain harmony and to avoid discord in the community.

About Division in the Community:
Certainly God did not punish any unruly tyrant in this world except after allowing him time and opportunity (for amends). The sufferings and misfortunes that have befallen you or that you have witnessed are enough for you to derive lessons. Not every man with a good heart is necessarily intelligent; not every ear listens, and not every eye sees (the truth).

I wonder about the faults of the groups who have introduced innovations in their religion, who do not follow the example of their Prophet nor emulate his successor. They do not believe in the unseen and do not abstain from evil. They are guided by their doubts and fall victim to their passions. They consider it good whatever they fancy, and consider it evil whatever they fancy. In dealing with complex issues, they make their own opinions (i.e., do not consult those with knowledge). They act as if each one of them is the Leader (Imam). Whatever they decide, they imagine it to be from a reliable source.
(Sermon 87)

When Facing a Rebellion:

There is no doubt that God sent down the Prophet as a guide with an eloquent Book. No one faces ruin except of one's own accord. Certainly only dubious innovations cause ruin. In God's authority lies the safety of your affairs. Therefore, obey Him in a sincere manner. By God, if you do not obey Him, He will take away the authority from you and bestow it upon another people.

These people dislike authority. If they succeed (in gaining power) despite their faulty views, the governmental system will be shattered. They strive (for power) out of jealousy against the leader, while God has bestowed His blessings and authority on him. Therefore, they intend to revert to the era of ignorance (i.e., the pre-Islamic period), whereas it is obligatory on me, for your sake, to abide by the Book of God (the Qur'an) and the teachings of the Prophet of God and to uphold his (the Prophet's) traditions (i.e., proclamations and actions). **(Sermon 168)**

ABOUT FAITH, DISBELIEF, AND DOUBT

Introduction: Imam Ali (p) had great insight into religion and the matters of faith. This was, in part, due to his closeness to the Prophet Muhammad (s), from whom he received knowledge and guidance. In this chapter, Imam Ali (p) shares his unique perspective on the subjects of faith (*Imaan*), disbelief (*Kufr*), and the causes of doubt and wavering of belief.[1]

Four Causes of Loss of Belief in God Are:

- Hankering after whims
- Passion to dispute every argument
- Deviation from truth
- Dissension (contentious disagreement)

Whoever hankers after whims does not incline towards truth. Whoever keeps on disputing every argument despite his ignorance will always remain blind to truth. Whoever deviates from truth because of ignorance will always mistake good for evil and evil for good, and he will remain intoxicated with misguidance. Whoever makes a breach (with God and His Messenger), his path becomes difficult, his affairs will become complicated, and his way to salvation will be uncertain.

Doubt:

Similarly, doubt has also four aspects:

- Absurd reasoning

---

1 These are excerpts from his sayings. For explanation, please refer to the section of abbreviations in the beginning of this book.

- Fear
- Vacillation
- Hesitation

(It leads to) easy surrender to infidelity, because one who has accustomed himself to unreasonable and absurd discussions will never see the light of truth and will always live in the darkness of ignorance. One who is afraid to face facts (of life, of death, and the life after death) will always turn away from the ultimate reality. One who allows doubts and uncertainties to vacillate him will always be under the control of Satan, and one who surrenders himself to infidelity earns damnation in both worlds (this life and the Hereafter).

When Imam Ali was asked about Faith in Religion, He Replied:

The structure of faith: It is supported by four pillars:

- Endurance
- Conviction
- Justice
- Struggle

Endurance:

It is composed of four attributes: eagerness, fear, God-consciousness, and anticipation (of death). Therefore, whoever is eager for Paradise will ignore temptations; whoever fears the fire of Hell will abstain from sins; whoever practices God-consciousness will easily bear the difficulties of life; and whoever anticipates death will hasten towards good deeds.

Conviction:

It has also four aspects:

- To guard oneself against infatuations of sin
- To search for explanation of truth through knowledge
- To gain lessons from instructive things

- To follow the precedent set by the people of previous generations

Whoever wants to guard himself against vices and sins will have to search for the true causes of infatuation, the true ways of combating them, and to find those true ways, to search with the help of knowledge.

Whoever is fully acquainted with various branches of knowledge will take lessons from life, and whoever tries to take lessons from life will engage in studying the causes for the rise and fall of previous civilizations.

Justice:
It also has four aspects:

- Depth of understanding
- Profoundness of knowledge
- Fairness of judgment
- Clearness of mind

Whoever tries his best to understand a problem will have to study it. Whoever has the practice of studying the subject he is to deal with will develop a clear mind and will always come to correct decisions. Whoever tries to achieve all this will have to develop ample patience and forbearance, and whoever does this has done justice to the cause of religion and has led a life of good repute and fame.

Struggle (*jihad*):
It is divided into four branches:

- To persuade people to be obedient to God
- To dissuade them from sin and vice
- To struggle (in the cause of God) sincerely and firmly on all occasions
- To detest the corrupt ones

Whoever persuades people to obey the orders of God provides strength to the believers. Whoever dissuades them from vices and sins humiliates the unbelievers. Whoever struggles persistently, he discharges all his obligations. He who detests the corrupt individuals for the sake of God, then God will take revenge on his enemies and he will earn God's good pleasure on the Day of Judgment.

When Asked about Patience, He Said:

Patience is of two kinds: patience over what causes you hurt, and patience against what you covet.

(Saying 31)

MISCELLANEOUS TOPICS

Introduction: Imam Ali (p) lived an extremely simple life, even as the ruler of the vast Islamic empire. He explains the reason for his lifestyle of extreme austerity, which does not imply being reclusive. Rather, it was a lifestyle whereby he avoided luxuries. He wore simple and inexpensive clothes, yet provided better clothes for his servants. He also ate meager food, yet provided better food to his servants.The reasons for these actions are explained in this chapter.

About a Learned Person:

The learned is the one who knows his worth. It is enough (reason) for a man to be (regarded) ignorant if he knows not his worth. Certainly the most disliked person with God is he whom God has left (alone) to his (selfish) self. He has gone astray from the right path and wanders about misguided. If he is called towards the worldly attractions, he is quick to respond, but if he is called to the bounties of the next world, he is not enthusiastic.

(Sermon 102)

About the Responsibilities of an Imam and Advice to Follow Him:

O people, secure light from the lamps (of guidance) of the preacher who practices what he preaches, and draw water from the spring which has been cleansed of impurities (i.e., a teacher who is purified of sins and worldly ambitions).

O creatures of God, do not rely on your ignorance; do not be obedient to your desires. Be God-conscious, and do not place your complaints before him who cannot redress your grievance.

Certainly there is no obligation on the Imam except the responsibility laid down on him by God, namely, to convey warnings, to exert in giving good advice, to revive the teachings of the Prophet (s), to enforce the religious law, and to issue the (fair) shares (of Charity) to the deserving. So hasten towards knowledge before it is too late, and before you lose touch with the teacher. Hold back others from the unlawful and abstain from it yourself, because you have been commanded to first abstain yourself before preaching to others.

(Sermon 104)

Certainly the (Divinely appointed) Imams are the vicegerents of God over His creatures, and they teach the people about God (and His commands).

(Sermon 151)

Those Who Will Go Astray:

With regard to me, two categories of persons will be ruined (go astray), namely, the one who loves me too much and the love takes him away from what is right, and the other who hates me much and the hatred takes him away from rightfulness. The best person with regard to me is he who takes the middle course. So be with the person who takes the middle course, and be with the majority (be united) because God's hand (i.e., protection) is on those who stay united. Beware of division, because a person isolated from the group is (prey) to Satan just as the isolated sheep from the flock is (prey) to the wolf.

(Sermon 126)

On Asceticism:

[A man complained to Imam Ali (p) about his brother and said, "He wears a (coarse) woolen coat and has cut himself away from the world." Imam Ali said, "Present him to me." When the man came, the Imam said as follows:]

O enemy of yourself! Certainly the evil one (Satan) has misguided you. Do you have no pity for your wife and your children? Do you believe that if you use those things which God has made lawful for you, He will dislike you? You are too unimportant for God to do so."

The man said: "O leader of the believers, you also put on coarse dress and eat meager food." Imam Ali replied, "Woe to you, I am not like you. Certainly God the Sublime has made it obligatory on true leaders that they should maintain themselves at the level of poor people so that the poor (subjects) do not bemoan over their poverty."
(Sermon 208)

10. HIS SELECTED SAYINGS REPLETE WITH WISDOM AND GUIDANCE

Sayings and Maxims of Imam Ali (p)

SAYINGS AND MAXIMS OF IMAM ALI (P)

Introduction: Translating idioms and sayings from the Arabic language into English is fraught with difficulties and imperfections. The selected maxims presented here from out of 480 maxims extracted from the book *Peak of Eloquence* have been rephrased in order to convey the essence and intent of what was said. It is hoped that the reader will benefit from the wisdom contained therein.

1. He who is greedy is disgraced; he who discloses his hardships, faces humiliation; he who has no control over his tongue debases himself.[1]
2. **Pearls**:

    - Avarice is disgrace.
    - Poverty often hinders an individual from arguing his case.
    - A poor man is a stranger in his own town.
    - Misfortune and helplessness are calamities.
    - Patience is bravery.
    - God-consciousness is the best weapon of defense.

3. The best companion is Submission to the Will of God; wisdom is the noblest heritage; knowledge is the best sign of distinction.
4. The mind of a wise man is the safest custody of secrets; cheerfulness is the key to friendship; patience will conceal many defects.
5. A self-admiring person earns the dislike of others; charity and almsgiving are the best remedies for ailments and calamities.

For explanation of the term "Saying", please refer to the section on abbreviations in the beginning of this book.

1. The numbering here is for convenience. Please refer to Appendix G for key to original numbering assigned to the sayings in the book *Peak of Eloquence, Nahjul Balagha*.

6. When this world favors a person, it ascribes to him the merits of others, and when it turns its face away from him, it snatches away from him his own merits.
7. Live amongst people in such a manner that if you die they weep over you, and if you are alive, they crave your company.
8. If you overpower your enemy, pardon him (by way of thankfulness to God) for enabling you to subdue him.
9. When (even small) blessings come to you, do not lose them through ungratefulness (to God).
10. He who gallops with loose reins collides with death.
11. Overlook the shortcomings of generous people, because if they fall, God will support them.
12. Failures are often due to timidity and fear; disappointments are due to bashfulness; hours of leisure pass away like summer clouds, therefore do not waste the opportunities for performing good deeds.
13. Giving relief to the distressed and helping the oppressed are means for atonement for great sins.
14. O son of Adam, when you see that your Lord, the Glorified, bestows His favors on you, while you (continue to) disobey Him, you should fear Him (i.e., that His Wrath may turn those blessings into misfortunes).
15. Expressions of your face may reveal your hidden thoughts.
16. The best way to serve God is not to make a show of it.
17. Beware! God has not exposed many of your sinful activities; it may appear to you as if He has forgiven you. (Likely, He is giving you time to repent.)
18. A virtuous person is better than the virtue, and a vicious person is worse than the vice.
19. Be generous but not extravagant; be frugal but not miserly.
20. The best wealth is to give up excessive desires.
21. The one who utters negative things about others will himself become target of scandal.

Statements in parentheses are for explanation, and not part of the text.

22. Optional prayers (Optional Salaat) cannot attain the pleasure of God when one ignores obligatory prayers (Salaat).[1]
23. A wise person thinks before he speaks, whereas a fool speaks before he thinks.
24. A fool's heart is at the mercy of his tongue, whereas a wise man's tongue is under the control of his heart (mind).
25. One of the companions of Imam fell ill. Imam Ali called upon him and gave him this advice: "Be thankful to God. He has made this illness a thing to atone for your sin, because a disease in itself does not bring rewards to anyone; it merely expiates one's sins. As far as reward is concerned, one has to earn it with his good thoughts and deeds. The Almighty Lord grants Paradise to his subjects on account of their God-consciousness and noble thoughts."
26. Blessed is the man who always keeps the life in the Hereafter in his thoughts, who remembers the Day of Judgment in all his deeds, and who is happy with the lot that God has destined for him.
27. Certainly the prize for you to aim for (in the Hereafter) is paradise, so do not sell yourself short (for pleasures of this world).
28. The sin that makes you sad and repentant is liked by God more than the good deed that makes you vain.
29. The value of a man depends upon his courage; his truthfulness depends upon his self-respect; and his chastity depends upon his sense of honor.
30. Success requires foresight and resolve; foresight requires thinking and planning.
31. The real forgiveness is to forgive while having the power to punish.
32. The help given after a request would be either out of a sense of self-respect or from fear of rebuke. (Therefore, it is better to help before the request comes.)
33. There is no greater wealth than wisdom and no greater poverty than ignorance. There is no greater heritage than good manners and no greater support than consultation.

---

1 For explanation, please refer to the Glossary section.

34. Patience is of two kinds: patience over what hurts you and patience against your (unfulfilled) desires.
35. Wealth turns a foreign land into a homeland and poverty turns one's native place into a foreign land.
36. Contentment is the capital that does not diminish.
37. Wealth is the fountainhead of passions.
38. Whoever warns you (against sin) is like one who gives you good tidings.
39. The tongue is a beast; if let loose, it devours.
40. Return greetings with greater warmth. Repay a favor with what is more. The initiator of a favor deserves greater merit.
41. To deny the needy is of greater shame than to give something small in charity.
42. If you cannot achieve your desire, then be contented with what you have.
43. An ignorant person will either overdo or be negligent in performing a task.
44. The wiser a person, the less he talks.
45. To be a leader, one should be knowledgeable, and practice it before preaching.
46. Every breath of yours is one more step towards death.
47. Acquire wisdom from whomever you can (even from an adversary).
48. Knowledge and wisdom are the privilege of the faithful, so obtain them, even from one who is lacking in faith.
49. The worth of an individual is in his achievements.
50. Strive to acquire these five qualities:

    i) Have hope in God alone.
    ii) Fear nothing more than sin.
    iii) Do not be ashamed to admit what you do not know.
    iv) Do not be ashamed (or be afraid) to learn a new thing.
    v) Acquire patience, because its relationship to faith is like that of "the head to the body."

51. One who presupposes to know everything will stay ignorant.

52. I value the cautious opinion of an older individual more than the valor of a youth.
53. I wonder at the person who loses hope of salvation while the door of repentance is still open.
54. There are two sources of deliverance from God's punishment. God addressed the Prophet Muhammad(s) and said, *"God is not to chastise them (sinners) while you (Prophet) are among them, nor is God to chastise them, while they still seek forgiveness"* (Qur'an Chapter 8, Verse 33).
55. Whoever keeps his affairs with God in proper order (being obedient to God), God will also put his affairs of the world in order. Whoever arranges affairs for his salvation (By virtuous acts), God will arrange his worldly affairs. Whoever warns himself (purifies his heart), God will be his protector.
56. Advice: "Do not lose hope in God's Mercy. At the same time do not take for granted immunity from His punishment."
57. Refresh your tired mind by indulging in sayings and words of wisdom.
58. The knowledge that remains merely on the tongue is superficial knowledge. The intrinsic (real) value of knowledge is realized when it is acted upon.
59. Do not pray to the Lord saying, "Lord! Protect me from (undergoing) temptations and trials," for there is none who is not tempted and tried. Beseech Him to guard you against such temptation that would lead you to sins. God says in His Book: *"Know that your wealth and children are temptations."* **(Qur'an Chapter 8, Verse 28)**
60. When asked what is good, he replied: "Good is not in having much wealth and progeny, but good is in possessing much knowledge, forbearance, and much worship of God; and to thank God for your good deed and to repent for your evil deed."
61. To sleep in a state of firm belief is better than to pray in a state of doubtfulness.
62. In regard to the following passage of the Qur'an: *"Verily, to God we belong and to Him do we return"* **(Qur'an Chapter 2, verse 156)**. Imam Ali explained, "Our declaring, '*we belong to God,*' indicates

that we accept Him as our Master and Owner, and when we say '*our return is to Him,*' it is an admission that we are mortal."

63. Someone praised Imam Ali. He replied, "God knows me best, and I know myself better than you do." Then he prayed, "O Lord! Make me better than what they think of me and excuse my weaknesses that they are not aware of."
64. Fulfillment of (others') needs becomes a lasting virtue in the following ways: "Regard it small so that it attains greatness, conceal it so that it may manifest itself, and give it in a timely manner so that it brings pleasantness."
65. Whoever likes to indulge in vain pleasures will dislike austerity, whereas salvation requires austerity.
66. Imam Ali (p) said this about people who wake up at night to offer prayers to God: "Those are the fortunate ones, for they take the Qur'an and the prayers as their guide and protector. Like Jesus Christ, they forsake the world and its vain pleasures. Prophet David had said that this was the hour when prayers are accepted."
67. Many educated people have ruined their Hereafter because of their ignorance of religion. Their (secular) knowledge was not of use to them.
68. No one can establish the rule of God (on earth) except an individual who, in enforcing justice, is neither deficient nor is weak. He is neither greedy nor a wrongdoer.
69. He who loves the family of the Prophet must be willing to lead an austere life.
70. **Pearls of wisdom:**

- No wealth is more profitable than wisdom.
- No loneliness is worse than one caused by one's vanity.
- No eminence is more exalted than God-consciousness.
- No trait is more useful than politeness.
- No heritage is better than good manners.
- No guidance is superior to the Divine guidance.
- No deal is more profitable than good deeds.
- No profit is greater than Divine reward.

- No abstinence is better than to be free from doubts (about religion).
- No virtue is better than refraining from prohibited deeds.
- No exaltation is superior to knowledge.
- No knowledge is superior to contemplation and prudence.
- No worship is more sacred than fulfillment of obligations (in religion).
- No belief is loftier than modesty and endurance.
- No eminence is greater than humility.
- No power is like one with forbearance.
- No support is stronger than consultation.

71. A good deed accompanied with God awareness is sure to be accepted.
72. Two kinds of people will go astray on my account: those who, in their opinions, exaggerate my position, and those who berate my position because of jealousy or malice.
73. A lost opportunity results in grief.
74. This world is like a serpent; it is soft to the touch, but full of poison. Naive people are attracted by it, but wise ones keep away from it.
75. There is a deed whose pleasure passes away (quickly), leaving behind pain and punishment, and there is a deed that, though unpleasant, earns divine reward.
76. Someone laughed loudly at a funeral. On hearing that, Imam Ali (p) remarked, "Is it that death is ordained only for others? Or are we exempt from it?"
77. **Blessed is the person**:

- Who humbles himself before God.
- Whose source of income is honest.
- Whose intentions are honorable.
- Whose character is noble.
- Who gives his wealth for the pleasure of God.
- Who restrains his tongue from vain talk.

- Who does not oppress.
- Who does not make innovations in religion.

78. **Imam Ali (p) passed by a cemetery. He stopped and gave an address in this manner:** "O resident of these abodes (Graves) where you are so lonely! O people of dust. O people of desolateness! You have gone ahead of us, but we are following you and shall meet you. The houses you left behind have been occupied by others. Your wives (widows) have married others. Your properties have been distributed among your heirs! This is the news from here. What is the news about things around you?"
79. **Pearls**

    - I wonder at a miser who chooses to lives like a destitute, but in the next world will have to give account like a rich person.
    - I wonder at the arrogant and vain person. Yesterday he was only a lowly sperm, and tomorrow he will be a corpse.
    - I wonder at the person who observes the universe created by God, yet doubts the existence of God.
    - I wonder at the person who sees people die, yet forgets his own end (death).
    - I wonder at the person who understands the marvel of the beginning of life, yet refuses to accept that he will be brought back to life again.
    - I wonder at the man who takes great pains to decorate his temporary habitat (of this world), yet ignores his permanent abode (the Hereafter).

80. Whoever has no share for God (charity) in his wealth, there is no place for him in God's Kingdom.
81. If you appreciate the Majesty of God, then you will attach less significance to lower beings.
82. If the people of the grave were to speak, they would inform you that the best provision for the next world is God-consciousness.

83. This world is not a permanent abode; it is like a highway, and you are a traveler.
84. A friend cannot be a (true) friend unless he is tested on three occasions: a) in time of one's need, b) behind one's back, and c) after one's death.
85. Daily (ritual) prayers are the best medium through which one may seek nearness to God.
86. Before praying to God for increase of sustenance, give something in charity.
87. A person who is sure of good returns shows generosity.
88. Help (from God) comes in proportion to needs.
89. He who practices moderation will not face poverty.
90. Loving one another is one-half of wisdom.
91. (God's) gift of endurance is in proportion to the difficulty.
92. Many individuals get nothing (spiritual) out of observing fasts, except hunger and thirst; many get nothing out of their night prayers but (physical) exertion and loss of sleep. The sleep and eating of an Intelligent (Godly) person is much better (more acceptable).
93. Fortify your faith with charity. Protect your wealth with the aid of *Zakaat* (obligatory Islamic charity). Ward off calamities by offering prayers.
94. An individual's worth is known through his speech.
95. One who does not know his own worth is condemned to failure.
96. Patience will ultimately lead to success.
97. One who agrees with the action of a group is regarded (by God) as having committed that action.
98. A man who participates in a sinful deed will be regarded as having committed two sins, one for committing the sin and the other sin for agreeing to it.
99. You have been shown (the good), if only you care to see; you have been given guidance, if only you care to heed; you have been counseled, if (only) you care to listen.
100. One who visits places of ill repute has no right to complain against a person who speaks ill of him.
101. One who acquires authority succumbs to favoritism.

102. One who guards his secrets has control over his affairs.
103. Vanity hinders progress.
104. Obsession to secure a gain becomes a hindrance to achieving many other gains.
105. One who strives for the sake of God receives His help.
106. Your advantage over others is in proportion to your knowledge and wisdom.
107. Counter an evildoer by rewarding a good-doer.
108. To remove evil from others, first give it up yourself!
109. Obstinacy hinders good advice.
110. Greed is (akin to) slavery.
111. To keep silent when you can say something wise and useful is as bad as promoting foolish ideas.
112. Death is never very far.
113. One who forsakes truth earns eternal damnation.
114. If you have collected (wealth) more than you need, then you (in reality) act as its trustee for someone else to use it (after your death).
115. Lack of gratitude (by a person) for your favor should not make you discouraged. There will be another person showing gratitude for much smaller favor. The reward for your goodness is with God.
116. Forbearance will make people side with you against the one who wronged you.
117. **The past is a good teacher for the following**:

    - One who derives lessons from the events of life thus gains vision; the vision makes him wise, and wisdom makes him gain knowledge.
    - One who is cognizant of his shortcomings will benefit from it, and one who is unmindful of his shortcomings will suffer consequences.
    - One who fears the Day of Judgment is safe from the punishment of God.

118. Happiness is to bear sorrows and calamities patiently.

119. Power leads to abuse.
120. Adversity shows one's mettle.
121. Jealousy betrays sincere friendship.
122. Greed dulls the faculties of judgment and wisdom.
123. Oppression earns the worst provisions in the Hereafter.
124. It is the highest act of nobility to ignore others' faults.
125. Advice:

    - Silence will earn respect and dignity.
    - Justice and fair play will make more friends.
    - Benevolence and charity will enhance prestige and status.
    - Courtesy will earn benevolence from others.
    - Service to humanity will secure leadership.
    - Good words will overcome powerful enemies.

126. A greedy person is (always) in the shackles of disgrace.
127. There are people who worship God to earn rewards; this is the worship of merchants. There are some who worship Him seeking safety from His punishment; this is the worship of slaves. A few worship God out of their sense of gratitude; their worship is that of the free and noble.
128. Every blessing carries a right of God. If one fulfills that right, then the blessing increases, but if one falls short, the blessing might be lost.
129. The sourness of this world is (in fact) sweetness of the next world, and sweetness of this world is bitterness of the next world.
130. Anger is akin to madness, and the person usually repents; if not, then the madness is confirmed.
131. Love your friend to a limit, for it is possible that one day he may turn into your enemy. Detest your enemy to a limit, for it is possible that one day he may become your friend.
132. When optional acts interfere with your obligatory acts, then omit the optional ones.

133. Even if there were no chastisement for disobedience, it would still be obligatory to obey God out of gratitude for His blessings.
134. God, the Glorified, has fixed the livelihood of the poor in the wealth of the affluent. Consequently, when a destitute one remains hungry, it is because some affluent person had denied him (his share). God, the Sublime, will question him (the affluent) about it.

135 **Gems about knowledge**

- Knowledge is of two kinds: one that is absorbed, and one that is not. The latter will not benefit unless absorbed
- Knowledge is better than wealth. Knowledge guards you, while you have to guard wealth.
- Wealth decreases by spending, while knowledge multiplies by spending.
- With knowledge, one commands obedience, and after death leaves a good name.
- Knowledge is ruler, while wealth is ruled upon.
- Knowledge calls for action, otherwise it departs.

136. Do not be one who regards others faults as significant, yet downplays his own faults.
137. Awareness of one's own shortcomings prevents one from looking into others'.
138. He who talks much commits more errors, and the one who knows that his words are a component of his actions is careful what he says.
139. Contentment is a capital that never dwindles. He who remembers death often is satisfied with receiving even small favors in this world.
140. The greatest defect in a person is to point out a defect in others while he has it himself.
141. Self-improvement is to avoid what you consider bad in others.

142. O people! Fear God; for a human is not created for naught to waste oneself away, nor to be left unaccounted to commit nonsensical acts.
143. Livelihood is of two kinds: the livelihood that you seek and the livelihood that seeks you. Even if you do not seek the latter, it will come to you.
144. Words are in your control before you utter them, but once you have uttered them, you are under their control. Therefore, guard your tongue as you guard your gold and silver. One expression may make you lose a blessing or invite punishment.
145. When you are strong, be strong in obedience to God, and when you are weak, be weak in committing sins.
146. Beware, destitution is a calamity; worse than destitution is ailment of the body; and worse than ailment of the body is ailment of the heart (soul).
147. Beware, wealth is a blessing; better is the health of the body, and (even) better than health of the body is purity of the heart.
148. Speak, so that you may be known. An individual is hidden behind his tongue.
149. Asking for forgiveness of God requires fulfilling the following six conditions:

    1. Repent for the sin committed.
    2. Make a firm determination not to repeat it.
    3. Discharge the rights of others.
    4. Fulfill the obligation ignored.
    5. Consume lawfully earned sustenance, so that the body is cleansed of (spiritual) defects.
    6. Make the body taste the hardship of obedience, as you had tasted the pleasures of disobedience.

150. Whoever sets right his/her inner self, God will set right the outward self. Whoever performs acts (of service) for the religion, God will provide him/ her with the needs of this world. If the dealings of an individual are good between himself and God,

then God will make the dealings good between that individual and other people.

151. Forbearance is like a covering (for the defects), and wisdom is like a sharp sword that kills excessive desires.

152. **The lovers of God:**

- They look at the inner side of things (while others look at the outer).
- They busy themselves with the lasting benefits (of the next world) while others seek immediate (worldly) benefits.
- They suppress those desires that they fear would hurt them (in the next world).
- They regard accumulation of wealth by others as a matter of lesser importance.
- They do not regard worldly hopes higher than their hope in the Hereafter.
- They do not regard worldly fear greater than the fear of disconnecting from God.

153. The worst sin is that which the committer takes lightly.

APPENDIX A

A Short Biography of the Author of the Book *Nahjul Balagha*, Imam[1] Ali bin Abu Talib (p)

Ali bin Abu Talib (p) was the Caliph, the cousin, and son-in-Law of Prophet Muhammad (s).

His birth: He was born in 600 AD within the holy precincts of the Kaba, the house of God in Mecca, Saudi Arabia.[2] Ali's father was Abu Talib, the chief of the noble Hashemite tribe and an uncle of the Prophet Muhammad (s). His mother was Fatima bint Asad, who came from a noble clan.

His early life: Prophet Muhammad raised Ali as a child and thereby a strong lifelong bond was formed between the two. When Prophet Muhammad (s) received his ministry at age forty, Imam Ali, who was then twelve years of age, was the first one to accept his invitation to Islam.

In the fourth year of his ministry, Prophet (s) invited his relatives (On divine instructions) to the worship of one God and informed them that he was a prophet of God. He was met with indifference and even ridicule. Ali came forward and pledged his allegiance to the Prophet, promising to defend him and the new faith. Prophet was pleased and declared Ali to be his supporter and successor. Those in attendance laughed and ridiculed the Prophet (s) and furthermore taunted Abu Talib (his father) by saying that he had just been commanded to listen to and obey his own son.

---

1 For meanings of the word "Imam," Please refer to the section of Glossary.

2 His mother, Fatima bint Asad, was a noble and pious woman. Experiencing labor pains, she walked towards the holy precinct of Kaba, whose door was locked. The wall of Kaba miraculously opened and she entered the holy sanctuary and the wall then closed. This was the only case of any pregnant woman having delivered within the holy precincts of Kaba in its recorded history.

Yet, true to his word, Ali protected, defended, and followed the Prophet (s) like a shadow, shielding him from enemies and being ever ready to give his life in the service of Islam.

To save Prophet's life, Ali slept on his bed: The idol worshippers of Mecca had plotted to kill Prophet Muhammad (s) in order to prevent his message of monotheism from spreading. The Prophet (s) was informed of the plot, and he decided to migrate (Known as Hijra, the beginning of Islamic calendar) to the neighboring city of Medina. He asked Ali, his young cousin, to sleep in his bed in order to distract and confuse the potential assassins and allow him time to leave Mecca. Imam Ali gladly accepted this responsibility, risking his life so that the Prophet's life would be saved.

City of Medina welcomes the Prophet: While Islam was taking a foothold in Medina, the Polytheists of Mecca waged several wars against Muhammad (s) in order to root out the new religion. Ali was in the forefront of defending the Prophet and was a key factor in defeating the enemy (in the defensive wars). His bravery and swordsmanship became proverbial in Arabia.

The Prophet weds his daughter to Ali: Prophet (s) had refused many proposals for his daughter (Fatima) from prominent and wealthy companions. He gladly accepted Ali's proposal to his daughter. He blessed the couple and prayed to God for their happiness and success. This event further increased mutual affection and closeness between Ali and the Prophet.

Pilgrimage of the Prophet: In the tenth year after Hijra, when the Prophet (s) was returning from his last pilgrimage (Hajj), he halted the journey at the parting place of the caravans and called back all those who had gone ahead and waited for those still behind. He then delivered what is known as "the Last Sermon." He forewarned that his end was near. Towards the end of this sermon, he declared, "The Almighty God is my *Maula* (A comprehensive word in Arabic, meaning master, protector and friend) and the *Maula* of all those who believe, and I am similarly the *Maula* of all those who believe, and I have more right over the believers' lives than they have on their own selves." Then he asked, "Do you believe in this claim?" All of them replied in the affirmative.

At this point, he solemnly declared, "Then hear and remember: of whomsoever I am *Maula*, this Ali is also his *Maula*! He is to me what Aaron was to Moses. O God, Be a friend to him who befriends him and enemy to him who opposes him! Help those who help him and frustrate those who frustrate him!" While he was saying these words, he raised Ali so that all those in the gathering may have a look at him.

This particular event has been recorded in Imam Ahmed ibn Hanbal's Musnad, verse 5, page 281, and Imam al-Ghazali's book *Sir-ul-Aalameen*. Maulana Askari Ja'fari states that 153 famous authors have recorded this event, known as Ghadeer-e-Khum, in their writings.

Ali as Caliph and Ruler: After the death of the third Caliph, Ali (p) was declared the Caliph by popular demand. During his administration, his top priority was to remove the corrupt regional governors of the Islamic empire. He demanded honesty, integrity, accountability, and compassion from the government officials. He himself adopted an extremely austere lifestyle.

When he appointed Malik-al-Ashtar as governor of Egypt, he instructed him in detail regarding his dealing with various classes of his subjects. He emphasized upon him the importance of being God-conscious, honest, just, and humble.

The famous Arab Christian scholar, jurist, and philosopher Abdul Maseeh Anthaki says that this order of Imam Ali established a far superior code of administration than the one handed down by Prophet Moses. He congratulated Ali for establishing those principles.

His code of administration, as documented in the book *Nahjul Balagha* (*Peak of Eloquence*), was quoted in the United Nations by the U.N. Secretary General in the year 2002 during a meeting of the Arab Development Fund. He advised the rulers and government officials to follow the principles contained therein as a role model of governance.

(Please refer to *Nahjul Balagha*, Letter No. 53, "An Order to Malik-al-Ashtar.")

During his brief rule of about six years, Ali had to deal with corruption and rebellion by some of his Governors and officials. He fought several wars to defend his principles and to maintain the integrity of the Muslim Empire. He died at the age of sixty-three after being mortally wounded by an enemy while he was praying in the mosque. His words when he was struck with the sword were: "I thank thee, O Lord, for rewarding me with martyrdom. How kind and Gracious of Thee. May Thy Mercies further me to the Glory of Thy realm."

His knowledge: His close association with the Prophet (s) enabled him to gain knowledge that no other person had. His vast field of knowledge included biology, medicine, astronomy, the origin of the universe (please refer to his famous sermon number one in *Nahjul Balagha*), philosophy, Islamic jurisprudence, mathematics, rhetoric, and more. He made major contributions to developing the grammar of the Arabic language.

Nahjul Balagha. The title of the book means *Peak of Eloquence*. It has sermons, letters, and sayings of Imam Ali (p). It was compiled by Syed Razi, and it is said that the subject matter contained therein is next only to the Qur'an in knowledge, eloquence, and guidance. Imam Ali's teachings are not only beneficial to Muslims but also to all human beings who are searching for truth and justice, and aspire for God-consciousness.

APPENDIX B

Statements of Prominent Scholars and Historians Regarding Imam Ali (p)

Ibn Abil Hadid: This well-known Egyptian commentator on the book *Nahjal Balagha (The Peak of Eloquence)* says that Ali had a personality in which opposing characteristics had so gathered themselves that it was difficult to believe that such a combination could manifest itself in a human being. He was the bravest man and boldest warrior that history could cite, and while such brave persons are usually hard-hearted, cruel, and bloodthirsty, instead Ali was kind, sympathetic, responsive, and a warmhearted person. These are the qualities of a pious and God-fearing person. He was friendly with the rich, poor, educated, and ignorant alike. He had a tender spot in his heart for everyone who was downtrodden, crippled, widowed, and orphaned. He was frequently seen smiling and giving happy greetings to others. He was known to be very witty and could not be overcome in debate.

Allamah Askari Ja'fari: A prominent scholar and translator of the book *Nahjul Balagha* says: "The world cannot quote an example, other than that of Ali, who was a first-class warrior and marshal, a philosopher and moralist, and a great teacher of religious principles and theology. The study of his life shows that his sword was the only help, which Islam received during its early days of struggle and wars of self-defense. For Islam, he was the first line of defense, the second line of defense, and the last line of defense."

Thomas Carlyle, *Scottish historian, critic, and sociological writer (1795–1881):* "As for this young Ali, one cannot but like him. A noble-minded creature, as he shows himself, now and always afterwards, full of affection, of fiery daring. (There was) something chivalrous in him; brave as a lion; yet with a grace, a truth, and affection worthy of Christian knighthood."

[*On Heroes, Hero-Worship, And the Heroic in History*, 1841, Lecture 2: The Hero as Prophet. Mahomet: Islam, May 8, 1840]

Edward Gibbon, *considered the greatest British historian of his time (1737–1794):* "The zeal and virtue of Ali were never outstripped by any recent proselyte. He united the qualifications of a poet, a soldier, and a saint; his wisdom still breathes in a collection of moral and religious sayings; and every antagonist, in the combats of the tongue or of the sword, was subdued by his eloquence and valour. From the first hour of his mission to the last rites of his funeral, the apostle (Muhammad) was never forsaken by a generous friend, whom, he delighted to name his brother, his vicegerent, and the faithful Aaron of a second Moses."

[*The Decline and Fall of the Roman Empire*, London, 1911, volume 5, pages 381–2]

Dr. Henry Stubbe, *classicist, polemicist, physician, and philosopher (1632–1676):* "He had a contempt of the world, its glory and pomp, he feared God much, gave many alms, was just in all his actions, humble and affable; of an exceeding quick wit and of an ingenuity that was not common, he was exceedingly learned, not in those sciences that terminate in speculations but those which extend to practice."

[*An Account of the Rise and Progress of Mahometanism*, 1705, page 83]

Charles Mills, *leading historical writer of his time (1788–1826):* "As the chief of the family of Hashim and as the cousin and son-in-law of him whom the Arabians respected...to the advantages of his birth and marriage was added the friendship of the Prophet. The son of Abu Talib was one of the first converts to Islamism and Mohammad's favourite appellation of his was the Aaron of a second Moses. His talents as an orator, and his intrepidity as a warrior, were grateful to a nation in whose judgment courage was virtue and eloquence was wisdom."

[*An History of Muhammedanism*, London, 1818, page 89]

Simon Ockley *professor of Arabic at the University of Cambridge (1678–1720):* "One thing particularly deserving to be noticed is that his mother was delivered of him at Mecca, in the very temple itself; which never happened to anyone else."

[*History of the Saracens*, London, 1894, page 331]

Washington Irving *well known as the "first American man of letters" (1783–1859):* "He was of the noblest branch of the noble race of Koreish. He possessed the three qualities most prized by Arabs: courage, eloquence, and munificence. His intrepid spirit had gained him from the prophet the appellation of The Lion of God, specimens of his eloquence remain in some verses and sayings preserved among the Arabs; and his munificence was manifested in sharing among others, every Friday, what remained in the treasury. Of his magnanimity, we have given repeated instances; his noble scorn of everything false and mean, and the absence in his conduct of everything like selfish intrigue." [*Lives of the Successors of Mahomet*, London, 1850, p. 165] "He indulged in the poetic vein himself, and many of his maxims and proverbs are preserved, and have been translated in various languages. His signet bore this inscription: 'The kingdom belongs to God.' One of his sayings shows the little value he set upon the transitory glories of this world, *'Life is but the shadow of a cloud—the dream of a sleeper.'* "

[*Lives of the Successors of Mahomet*, London, 1850, pages 187-8]

Robert Durey Osborn, *major of the Bengal Staff Corps (1835–1889):* "With him perished the truest hearted and best Moslem of whom Mohammadan history had preserved the remembrance."

[*Islam Under the Arabs*, 1876, page 120]

Allamah Masoodi, *well-known historian of Islam:* "If the glorious name of being the first Muslim, a comrade of Prophet in exile, his faithful companion in the struggle for the faith, his intimate associate in life, his kinsman, with a true knowledge of his (Prophet's) teachings, including the book (the Qur'an); if self-abnegation, the practice of justice; if honesty, purity, the love of truth;

if knowledge of Law and science, constitute a claim to pre-eminence, then all must regard Ali as the foremost Muslim. We shall search in vain to find, either among his predecessors (except Prophet Muhammad), or among his successors, those virtues that God had endowed him with."

Dr. Ata Mohy-ud-Din: "Ali was the man of many and varied talents, one of the greatest savants, legislators, generals, statesmen, scholars, and administrators the world has ever known. In his person he combined the knowledge of Adam (the Prophet), the virtue of Noah, the devotion of Abraham, the awe and majesty of Moses, the abstinence and piety of Jesus Christ, the patience and resignation of Job, the wisdom of Solomon, the prowess of Alexander (the great), the iron determination of Julius Caesar, the sagacity and prudence of Plato, the scholastic accomplishment of Cicero and the reformative zeal of Justinian."

[*Ali the Superman*, by Dr. Ata Mohy-ud-Din. Muhammad Ashraf Publishers, Lahore, Pakistan 1980]

George Jordac: "Ali formulated such firm rules and presented such solid views for the rights of human beings and the welfare of the human society, that their roots penetrate into the depths of earth and their branches extend up to the heavens."

[In the book *The Voice of Human Justice*, by George Jordac, page 83]

APPENDIX C

A Word about the Compiler of Nahjul Balagha, Syed Mohammad Razi

Syed Razi compiled the sermons, letters, and sayings of Imam Ali (p) in Arabic, the original language, about one thousand years ago. This was about four hundred years after the death of Imam Ali.

Syed Razi was born in the city of Baghdad, in Iraq, in the Islamic calendar year 359 AH (969 AD.) He traced his lineage to Prophet Muhammad (s). He came from a noble family of scholars. His early education was under the tutelage of renowned scholar and theologian Shaikh Mofeed. Subsequently, he joined several institutions, the most notable of which was run by Abu Ishaq Ahmed ibn Mohammad Tabari. His subjects included the Qur'an, the Hadith (i.e., traditions and teachings of Prophet Muhammad), history of religions, philosophy, and literature. He was considered a prodigy by the scholars of his time. During his short lifespan of forty-seven years, he wrote many books. His commentary on the Qur'an is highly acclaimed by scholars.

Since his early age, he was interested in the writings and teachings of Imam Ali (p). Some of the earlier collected works of Imam Ali's teaching had been lost. Syed Razi decided to recollect them. He traveled great distances to collect the sermons, letters, and sayings of Imam Ali, classifying them under those three headings, and gave the compilation the title of *Nahjul Balagha* (i.e., *Peak of Eloquence*). Despite failing health, his passion made him spend long hours each day for several years to collect the material. He made the utmost effort to guarantee the authenticity of the original writings.

Before his death, Syed Razi left behind some forty books written by him. Some of them are considered great literary and scholarly works, and perhaps none more so than *Nahjul Balagha*.

APPENDIX D

Names of Prophets and other terms in the Qur'an (Arabic) with corresponding names in the Bible (English):

ARABIC	ENGLISH	ARABIC	ENGLISH	ARABIC	ENGLISH
Ayyub	Job	***Idrees***	Enoch	***Nuh***	Noah
Al-Yasa	Elisha	***Maryam***	Mary	***Qarun***	Korah
Dawood	David	***Isma'il***	Ishmael	***Saba***	Sheba
Fir'aun	Pharaoh	***Isa***	Jesus	***Sulei-man***	Solomon
Haroon	Aaron	***Jibreel***	Gabriel	***Taurat***	Torah
Ibrahim	Abraham	***Jaloot***	Goliath	***Uzair***	Ezra
Imran	Amran	***Lut***	Lot	***Taloot***	Saul
Ilyas	Elias	***Majuj***	Magog	***Yahya***	John the Baptist
Injeel	Evangel, Gospel	***Mika'il***	Michael	***Yunus***	Jonah
Ishaq	Isaac	***Musa***	Moses	***Yusuf***	Joseph
Yaqub	Jacob	***Zakariyya***	Zachariah	***Aadam***	Adam
Hud	Eber				

APPENDIX E

Below are the sermon numbers quoted in this book showing the respective titles of the sermons in the original work *Peak of Eloquence (Nahjul Balagha)*

Sermon Number*	Title of the Sermon**
1.	Creation of Earth and sky
2.	Arabia before prophet
12.	Victory over enemy
45.	God's greatness, lowliness of world
48.	While marching towards Syria
64.	God's Attributes
80.	About preaching and counseling
82.	It is called "al-Gharra," a wonderful sermon
84.	Perfection of God
85.	Preparation for the next world
89.	God's Attributes and his advice
90.	Sermon of "Skeletons," In praise of God
93.	Praise of God and eulogy of Prophets
99.	Prophet Muhammad (s) and his descendants
108.	About the Might of God
113.	Abstemiousness, God-fearing, and preparing for the next world
130.	About caliphate and qualities of a ruler
131.	About God, the Qur'an, the Prophet, and this world
141.	Misplaced generosity
154.	Wonderful creation of bat
159.	Greatness of God, hope and fear
162.	Attributes of God
163.	Wonderful creation of peacock

166.	Fulfillment of Rights and Obligations
175.	Preaching about the Qur'an, good and bad deeds
176.	In answer to question, if he had seen God.
181.	God's praise, His bounties, Day of Judgment
184.	Oneness of God, his expounding of knowledge
185.	Vicissitude of times
187.	Firm and shaky beliefs, urging people to learn from him
190.	About God-consciousness, world and its people
191.	Sermon of disparagement
194.	Day of Judgment, transience of this world
197.	God's Omniscience, degrees of God-consciousness
198.	Advice to his companions
210.	Greatness of God, creation of universe
212.	God's sublimity, Prophet's eulogy
215.	Mutual rights of the ruler and the ruled
220.	Glorify God, remember Him day and night, and fear Day of Judgment

---

***Sermon numbers may have slight discrepancies in different editions of *Nahjul Balagha*. The above numbering is from www.nahjulbalagha.com.**

****For the sake of brevity, full title may not be displayed.**

APPENDIX F

The Letter numbers quoted in this book with their respective titles in the original work *Peak of Eloquence, Nahjul Balagha**

Letter number	Title of Letter**
1.	Instruction to Marshal heading for battle
12.	Instruction to soldiers before a battle
14.	Instruction to soldiers before battle of Siffin
15.	Prayer when facing an enemy
16.	Instructions to his followers in a battle
18.	Letter to Governor of Basra
19.	Advice to governors regarding God's laws
20.	To an official about misappropriation of funds
22.	Beneficial advice to his uncle
23.	Instructions to his family, anticipating death
25.	Instructions to *Zakat* (tax) collectors
26.	More instructions to tax collectors
27.	Instructions to a new governor
29.	To people of province of Basra
31.	Advice to his son, when returning from a battle
38.	Letter to people of Egypt
41.	Letter to a delinquent governor
45.	Instructions to his envoy
77.	Instructions to his negotiator sent to rebellious people
79.	To governor of Basra
46.	Letter to one of his governors
50.	A circular issued to army officers
51.	Letter to tax and revenue collectors
53.	Letter to the newly appointed governor of Egypt

55.	Letter to a rebellious governor
57.	Letter to people of a province with weak loyalty
58.	Letter to people explaining reason for the battle of Siffin
59.	Letter to a governor
62.	Letter to people of Egypt, at appointment of new governor
67.	Letter to Governor of Makkah
69.	Advice to an individual
72.	Letter to a relative
76.	Instructions to his representative when sent to people of Basra province
77.	Instructions to his negotiator when sent to deal with rebels
79.	Orders issued to his generals at the beginning of his rule

---

***Adapted from www.nahjulbalagha.com.**

****For the sake of brevity, some of the titles are simplified.**

APPENDIX G

The serial numbers in "Sayings and Maxims of Imam Ali (p)," are for sake of convenience. Listed next to them in parentheses are the corresponding "sayings numbers" in the reference book *Peak of Eloquence, Nahjul Balagha,* published by Tahrike Tarsile Qur'an, Inc.

1(2), 2 (3, 4), 3 (5), 4 (6), 5 (6), 6 (9), 7 (10), 8 (11), 9 (13), 10 (19), 11 (20), 12 (21), 13 (24), 14 (25), 15 (26), 16 (28), 17 (30), 18 (32), 19 (33), 20 (34), 21 (35), 22 (39), 23 (40), 24 (41), 25 (42), 26 (44), 27 (465), 28 (46), 29 (47), 30 (48), 31 (52), 32 (53), 34 (55), 35 (56), 36 (57), 37 (58), 38 (59), 39 (60), 40 (62), 41 (67), 42 (69), 43 (70), 44 (71), 45 (73), 46 (74), 47 (79), 48 (80), 49 (81), 50 (82), 51 (85), 52 (86), 53 (87), 54 (88), 55 (89), 56 (90), 57 (97), 58 (92), 59 (93), 60 (94), 61 (97), 62 (99), 63(100), 64 (101), 65 (103), 66 (104), 67 (107), 68 (110), 69 (112), 70 (113), 71 (95), 72 (117), 73 (118), 74(119), 75 (121), 76 (122), 77 (123), 78 (130), 79 (126), 80 (127), 81 (129), 82 (130), 83 (133), 84 (134), 85 (136), 86 (137), 87 (138), 88 (139), 89 (140), 90 (142), 91 (144), 92 (145), 93 (146), 94 (148), 95 (149), 96 (153), 97 (154), 98 (154), 99 (157), 100 (159), 101 (160), 102 (162), 103 167), 104 (171), 105 (174), 106 (176), 107 (177), 108 (178), 109 (179), 110 (180), 111 (182), 112 (187), 113 (188), 114 (192), 115 (204), 116 (206), 117 (208), 118 (213), 119 (216), 120 (217), 121 (218), 122 (219), 123 (221), 124 (222), 125 (224), 126 (226), 127 (238), 128 (245), 129 (252), 130 (256), 131 (278), 132 (289), 133 (300), 134 (338), 135 (147, 348, 376), 136 (150), 137 (359), 138 (359), 139 (359), 140 (363), 141 (375), 142 (380), 143 (389), 144 (391), 145 (393), 146 (398), 147 (398), 148 (402), 149 (426), 150 (432).

GLOSSARY

Allah	Proper name of God in Arabic Qur'an.
Al-Ghazali	Abu Hamid Muhammad Al-Ghazali (1058–1111 AD) He was a renowned Muslim scholar, philosopher, and Sufi. He left behind some seventy books on varied subjects to his credit.
Ahmed bin Hanbal	Imam Ahmed bin Hanbal was founder of the Hanbali school of Islam. His manual of religious law is called "Musnad of Imam Hanbal."
Believer	The word in Arabic is *Mu'min.* It is a comprehensive word. Space does not permit to give all shades of its meanings. Briefly, a person who believes in God Almighty and does not associate a partner with Him, and acknowledges the prophet of God of his/her time (and the past prophets of God), and practices the religion according to the teachings of the revealed scripture brought by the prophet. For further reading, please refer to chapter 23 ("The believers") of the Qur'an.
Caliphate	Office of a Caliph (successor of Prophet Muhammad).
Coveting the world	Islamic teachings permit enjoying the gifts of God (in moderation), but do not be attached to them.

Day of Judgment	In Arabic, it is called *"Qiyamah."* Other terms used for it are Day of reckoning, the Hour, Resurrection, Armageddon, etc.
Divine Attributes	God's Attributes (also known as His Names) in the Qur'an.
Essence of God	The true knowledge about God.
Ghadeer-e-Khum	A pond in Saudi Arabia near Mecca at a place called Khum. Prophet Muhammad (s) delivered his last sermon while returning from Hajj pilgrimage.
God-conscious	A person who is aware of God's presence all the time. A pious person.
Hereafter	The Otherworldly existence that will follow the doomsday.
Hypocrites	In the time of Muhammad, those who outwardly embraced Islam, but in reality, they were hostile to the new faith. As "insiders," they plotted to weaken the faith community.
Ibn	"Son of."
Imam	This Arabic word means a religious leader. This title may be conferred by God (spiritual leader), or a person may be selected by the people by virtue of his Knowledge and God-consciousness. Imam of a congregation is the one who leads the congregational prayers (*Salaat*).
Jinn	These are ethereal creatures mentioned in the Qur'an. They are invisible to humans. Satan belongs to this category. Satan is not an angel, according to the Qur'an.

Ka 'aba	House of God in Mecca, Saudi Arabia. It is a cubicle approximately fifty feet by fifty feet by fifty feet. This symbolic structure is practically empty from inside. It was first built by the Prophet Adam (p), and then rebuilt by the Prophet Abraham. When praying, Muslims face toward it.
Knowledge of God	God's knowledge is all-inclusive; that of past, present, future, manifest and hidden. It is beyond human comprehension.
Knowledge of the Hour	Knowing when this world will come to an end and the Day of Judgment begins
Maula	It is an Arabic word, meaning master, protector, and friend.
Me'raj	The night of ascension. During his ministry, one night Angel Gabriel came on God's command and took prophet Muhammad (s) to higher heavens. God shared some of His secrets with Muhammad. Majority of Muslim scholars believe it was a physical journey. A small minority of the scholars believe it was a vision that Muhammad had. For details, please log on to **http://www.al-islam.org/al-miraj/.**
Monotheism in the Qur'an	It means that God is one and is indivisible. He has no partners, no associates, no helpers, no consort, no father and no son. He is uncreated, and everything else was created by Him. He is Eternal with no beginning and no end. He is Omnipotent and omniscient, and is high above what they ascribe to Him. When

He intends a thing, he says to it "Be," and "it is."

Mountains as pegs

"We have placed in the ground (mountains) standing firm, so that it does not shake with them" (Qur'an 21:31).

"Have We not made the earth an expanse and the mountains stakes (pegs)?" (Qur'an 78:6–7)

Peak of Eloquence

English translation of the title of the book *Nahjul Balagha*

Prayer

It has two meanings: 1) Ritual act of worship in Arabic known as "*Salaat.*" 2) Supplication.

Qur'an

Holy scripture revealed by God to the Prophet Muhammad (s) through Angel Gabriel. In the west, it is also known as "Koran."

Salaat

Canonical daily prayers performed in a defined ritual fashion five times a day. Additionally, optional prayers may be performed before or after the obligatory prayers, or at other times.

Satan

In Arabic he is known as "*Shaytaan.*" His proper name in the Qur'an is *"Iblees." He is also known as* Lucifer in English. He was created from fire and is a Jinn. God promised that he would be doomed to Hell's fire on the Day of Judgment because of his vanity and for disobeying God. Satan had no intention of repentance whatsoever; instead, he asked for certain requests and received them.

	Some of these included a lifespan until the day of resurrection, the ability to recruit comrades, ability to seduce and misguide humans through prompting in the heart. He seduces humankind by introducing a sense of superiority in relation to others, nurturing vain desires, greed, and much more. God promised that those who follow Satan will also be punished along with him. God says this in the Qur'an about Satan: "*(Satan) whom God has cursed and he (Satan) said:"Most certainly I will take an allotted share of Your servants. Surely, I will lead them astray and stir vain desires in them*" (Qur'an 4:118-119).
Syed Muhammad Razi	Original compiler of the book *Nahjul Balagha*.
Syed Ali Raza	Translated *Nahjul Balagha* in English
Throne of God	It is a metaphorical term. The whole universe is His Throne or seat.
Tradition (Hadith)	The proclamations, sayings, and teachings of Prophet Muhammad (s). With these and with the laws and guidance in the Qur'an, Muslims have a comprehensive system to follow in all aspects of their lives.

References:

Imam Ali ibn Abu Talib. *Peak of Eloquence, Nahjul Balagha*. Sermons, Letters and Sayings. Translated by Sayed Ali Reza. Elmhurst, New York: Tahrike Tarsile Qur'an, Inc., 1996. Website: www.koranusa.org.

Ali, Hazrat. *Nahjul Balagha*. Lake Mary, Florida. Sermons, Letters and sayings. Translated by Syed Mohammed Askari Jafery. Elmhurst, New York: Tahrike Tarsile Qur'an. Inc.

Imam Ali bin Abu Talib. *Nahjul Balaagha*. (Arabic text with English translation). Ahlul-Bayt Assembly of America: Potomac, Maryland, 1996 www.nahjulbalagha.com.

What Non-Muslims say about Imam Ali, www.al-islam.org.
Ahmed Ali, S.V. Mir. ***The Holy Koran Interpreted* . Lake Mary, Florida: United Muslim Foundation, 1996. www.islamquery.com.**

Suggested Reading

1. *The Voice of Human Justice*, by George Jordac. Ansariyan Publications, Iran. 1990
2. *Ali the Superman*, by Dr. Ata Mohy-ud-Din. Muhammad Ashraf Publishers, Lahore, Pakistan. 1980
3. *Justice and Remembrance, Introducing the spirituality of Imam Ali*, by Reza Shah-Kazemi. Published by I.B.Tauris & Co. Ltd., London, New York. 2007
4. *The Brother of Prophet Muhammad, the Imam Ali*, by Mohammad Jawad Chirri. Published by The Islamic Center of Detroit, 15571 Joy Road, Detroit, Michigan, 2000
5. *The Political and Moral Vision of Islam*, by S.M. Jafri. Published by Tahrike Tarsile Qur'an, Inc. Elmhurst, New York, 2009

INDEX

G

H

K

L

N

O

P

U

V

W

Y

Z

"By God, even if I am given all the domain of the Heavens, with all that exists under the skies, in order to disobey God to the extent of snatching one grain of barley from an ant, I will not do it. For me all (the riches of) the world are (worth) less than the leaf in the mouth of a locust that it is chewing."

[Imam Ali (p) in *Nahjul Balagha,* Sermon 222]